Rutgers University Studies in History

Volume I

# James Madison
## Philosopher of the Constitution

# James Madison

## *Philosopher of the Constitution*

*by*

Edward McNall Burns

*With a new preface and a new chapter (IV) by the author*

1968
OCTAGON BOOKS, INC.
*New York*

*Reprinted 1968*
*by special arrangement with Rutgers University Press*
OCTAGON BOOKS, INC.
175 Fifth Avenue
New York, N. Y. 10010

Library of Congress Catalog Card Number: 67-18757

*Printed in U.S.A. by*
NOBLE OFFSET PRINTERS, INC.
NEW YORK 3, N. Y.

To the memory of

EDWARD SAMUEL CORWIN

Profound Student of Political Thought

# Contents

# Preface
## to the Octagon Edition

THE original edition of this book was published in 1938. Since then much additional work has been done on the fourth President of the United States. An outstanding example is the monumental biography by Irving Brant. Adrienne Koch has included brilliant interpretative studies in her *Jefferson and Madison: The Great Collaboration* and *The American Enlightenment*. Finally, a new source material has been made available by William T. Hutchinson and William M. E. Rachal in their *Madison Papers,* of which the University of Chicago Press has already published four volumes.

The present edition of *James Madison: Philosopher of the Constitution* includes a new chapter entitled Republicanism. Its purpose is to emphasize more clearly the mixture of conservatism and liberalism that made up the philosophy of most of the Founding Fathers, Madison especially. They desired a government more truly representative of the people than the government of any other major country in the world at that time. Yet they feared the masses and strove to set limits to an effective exercise of majority rule. They believed in a wide extension of the franchise—even Alexander Hamilton advocated manhood suffrage—but they did not trust the people to elect the President directly or the members of the Senate. They insisted that government must rest upon the whole body of the people, but their system of checks and balances was designed to curb the power of the legislative branch, particularly of the House of Representatives. Their ideal of a republican system focused upon limited government; yet they did not consider a powerful executive and a judiciary with a veto upon "unwise" as well as unconstitutional legislation incompatible with this ideal. Their devotion to individual rights was unsurpassed in their time, but with the exception of Madison—and he was not always an exception—individual rights meant primarily the rights of property.

Many of Madison's most valuable contributions to political theory are contained in the *Federalist*, which he wrote in collaboration with Hamilton and John Jay. At the time I prepared the first edition of this book the authorship of several numbers of the *Federalist* was in dispute. I followed the practice of crediting Madison with all of those numbers he claimed to have written, on the assumption that since he claimed to have been the author of them, he must have agreed with their contents. This assumption was vindicated in April-July, 1944, when Douglass Adair published "The Disputed Authorship of the Federalist Papers," in the *William and Mary Quarterly*.

The preparation of this study would not have been possible without the wise suggestions and valuable criticism of many of my friends and associates. To Professors Edward S. Corwin of Princeton, Elmer D. Graper, B. H. Williams, M. R. Gabbert, and Alfred P. James of the University of Pittsburgh, L. Ethan Ellis of Rutgers University, and James C. Charlesworth of the

University of Pennsylvania my debt of gratitude is especially heavy. For the new edition I have benefited from the advice of Professor Leland D. Baldwin, formerly of the University of Pittsburgh and the University of California, Santa Barbara. The late Professor Corwin suggested this study, and most of the others read the manuscript in its entirety with results of immeasurable advantage to the author. I am grateful also to the librarians in charge of the manuscript divisions of the New York Public Library, the Columbia University Library, the Princeton University Library, and the Library of Congress for courteous and helpful services, and to my wife for her loyal support and faithful assistance with irksome detail.

EDWARD MCNALL BURNS

*Santa Barbara, California*
*October, 1967*

# Foreword

FOR reasons not altogether easy to understand the political philosophy of James Madison has received slight recognition. Professor Parrington, in his three volume work on *Main Currents in American Thought*, devotes a chapter each to John Adams and Daniel Webster, but dismisses the Father of the Constitution with eighteen casual references. Most other histories of American thought likewise give but scanty attention to Madison. I have endeavored in the pages that follow to give as complete an exposition and analysis of Madison's theories as possible, and also to show something of their influence and importance.

Some of Madison's most valuable contributions are contained in the *Federalist*, which he wrote in collaboration with Hamilton and Jay. Unfortunately the authorship of particular numbers of this series is still in dispute and will possibly never be settled. I have followed the practice of crediting Madison with all of those numbers which he claimed to have written, on the assumption that since he claimed to have been the author of them, he must at least have agreed with their contents. The conflicting views of the problem of authorship are discussed by E. G. Bourne in volume II of the *American Historical Review*, and by Henry Cabot Lodge in his edition of the *Federalist.*

The preparation of this study would not have been possible without the wise suggestions and valuable criticisms of many of my friends and associates. To Professors Edward S. Corwin of Princeton, Elmer D. Graper, B. H. Williams, M. R. Gabbert, and Alfred P. James of the University of Pittsburgh, and Ethan Ellis of Rutgers University my debt of gratitude is especially heavy. The first named suggested this study, and all have read the manuscript in its entirety with results of immeasurable advantage to the author. I am grateful also to the assistants in charge of the manuscript divisions of the New York Public Library, the Columbia University Library, the Princeton University Library, and the Library of Congress for courteous and helpful services, and to my wife for her loyal support and faithful assistance with irksome detail.

EDWARD McNALL BURNS

*New Brunswick, New Jersey*
*May, 1938*

# James Madison
# Philosopher of the Constitution

ONE

# Biographical Introduction

JAMES MADISON, "Father of the Constitution," and fourth President of the United States, was born March 16, 1751, the son of James and Nellie Conway Madison of Montpellier, Orange County, Virginia. The Madison family was an old one, relatively prosperous and conservative. James Madison Sr. owned slaves in considerable number, was vestryman of St. Thomas' parish, and a lay delegate to the Episcopal Convention of 1776.[1] A cousin of the same name became president of the College of William and Mary and the first Episcopal bishop of Virginia.[2]

The environment into which young Madison was born had precisely the character necessary to produce that peculiar combination of democratic and aristocratic inclinations that was to dominate the genius of the future statesman and philosopher. The counties of the Piedmont section, including Orange and Albemarle, the homes of Madison and Jefferson, respectively, were "strongholds of democracy."[3] Here were the principal centers of revolt against entails and primogeniture, against slavery and the Established Church. The section had the plantation system as its basis, but it was far from being the exclusive economic

[1] Gaillard Hunt, *The Life of James Madison*, New York, 1902, pp. 10-11.

[2] *Ibid.*, p. 11.

[3] Charles H. Ambler, *Sectionalism in Virginia from 1776 to 1861*, Chicago, 1910, p. 8.

pattern. Many of the farms were small. Wheat, flax, and corn had become staples of production in addition to tobacco. The population consisted largely of comparatively new families, many of whom were the descendants of Northern immigrants and poorer whites who had been forced out of the Tidewater. Although nearly twice as large as the Tidewater, the Piedmont had a much smaller number of negro slaves.[1]

So far the influences were on the side of democracy. But they do not tell the whole story. James Madison might almost be said to have inherited ruling class instincts. In the midst of a population composed largely of yeoman farmers, his father was the owner of an extensive plantation. He was in fact probably the largest landholder in the county; and as property conferred the chief title to distinction, he was the most important man in the community. He served as chairman of the county committee and county lieutenant, as well as vestryman of the parish. Since James Madison Jr. was the oldest son, under the rule of primogeniture then still in force, upon attaining his majority he was immediately regarded as the heir to the estate and entitled to share with his father the responsibilities and consideration of the head of an aristocratic family.[2]

The formal education of the young Madison was first of all entrusted to one Donald Robertson, a Scotsman with a reputation for extensive learning. The course of instruction included Latin, Greek, arithmetic, geography, algebra, geometry, and miscellaneous literature. After three or four years of this Madison studied for a year or two

[1] *Ibid.*, p. 8.

[2] Hunt, *op. cit.*, pp. 22-23.

longer under the Reverend Thomas Martin, the parish minister of the Established Church. In the meantime he appears to have done considerable reading on his own account. One of the first books to lure his interest was the *Spectator*, which he decided to be "peculiarly adapted to inculcate in youthful minds just sentiments, an appetite for knowledge, and a taste for the improvement of the mind and manners."[1] To what extent he may have profited from further intellectual adventures in his father's library, it is impossible to say. The collection included such captivating titles as *Warning to a Careless World*, *The Life of Man in the Soul of God*, and *The Nature of Sin*; but, significantly, also *Moses Unveiled*, *The Religion of Nature*, *Discourses on Quicksilver*, *The Motion of Fluids*, and Chambers' *Dictionary of Arts and Sciences*.[2]

In the year 1769 Madison was considered ready for college. For reasons which are not altogether clear, it was decided to send him to the College of New Jersey at Princeton instead of to William and Mary, the alma mater of most of the scions of the plantation aristocracy. Madison himself explained in his *Autobiography* that the climate at Williamsburg was considered unhealthful for persons coming from regions of higher altitude. It seems probable, however, that dissension at the time between the board of visitors and the faculty of William and Mary, and the unpopularity of the president had something to do with the choice of a different school.[3] It may also be that the selection was determined in part by the reputation which

[1] *Autobiography*, unpublished manuscript, Library of Congress.

[2] Manuscript, *Madison Papers*, Library of Congress.

[3] William C. Rives, *History of the Life and Times of James Madison*, Boston, 1881, vol. I, p. 17.

the college at Princeton was rapidly acquiring as the most progressive institution of liberal studies in America. Its president, the famous Dr. Witherspoon, had just recently inaugurated a series of curricular reforms introducing, among others, courses in history and the general principles of public law and politics.[1]

Only a few facts are known about Madison's career as a student at Princeton. His favorite subjects were those that related to the history of political institutions, although the curriculum as a whole was based chiefly on the classics and metaphysics, with constant practice in oratory.[2] He earned a reputation for amazing assiduity, restricting himself for a considerable period to less than five hours sleep out of the twenty-four.[3] Among his associates in college were several whose names were destined to become famous —Philip Freneau, Hugh Henry Brackenridge, Aaron Burr, and Henry Lee. In collaboration with a number of these, Madison founded the American Whig Society, for the purpose of "cultivating literature, friendship, and morality among the members."[4]

In 1771 Madison received his A.B. degree, having completed the three year course in two years. But the strain had so impaired his health that he had to secure exemption from attendance at commencement and did not feel able to return to Virginia.[5] He decided to spend the succeeding year in Princeton pursuing advanced studies in

[1] *Ibid.*, vol. I, p. 17.

[2] *Princeton University Alumni Records*, compiled by V. L. Collins, unpublished.

[3] *Autobiography*.

[4] Hunt, *op. cit.*, p. 15.

[5] *Autobiography*.

Hebrew and ethics. Gaillard Hunt concludes from this that Madison contemplated entering the ministry,[1] but there is no evidence of any such intention in his correspondence or other writings. He may have been motivated rather by an ambition to make his own learning embrace as many fields of knowledge as possible. His profound seriousness of purpose would seem to point to such a conclusion. Besides he maintains in his *Autobiography* that the law was already his chosen profession, apparently as the logical avenue to a career in public affairs. It is certain, however, that theology remained a correlative interest for two or three years. Among his early manuscripts are detailed and elaborate notes on the Gospels and the Acts of the Apostles and on such subjects as the Foreknowledge of God.[2]

In 1772 Madison returned to his father's plantation in Virginia, still in delicate health. There followed a period of about three years of melancholy and indecision. Brooding over the state of his health, he came to the conclusion that he was not long for this world.[3] The state of his mind was such that he could develop no interest in further preparation for the law, but at the same time he shrank from the associations of a Southern planter's life with its dependence upon slavery. To console his troubled spirit, he plunged into omnivorous reading and abstruse otherworldly speculations.[4]

[1] Hunt, *op. cit.*, p. 16.

[2] Rives, *op. cit.*, vol. I, pp. 33-34.

[3] Letter to William Bradford, Nov. 9, 1773, Gaillard Hunt, *The Writings of James Madison*, New York, 1900, vol. I, pp. 10-11; hereafter cited as *Writings* (Hunt ed.).

[4] Hunt, *Life of Madison*, p. 17.

The crux of events in the outside world put an end to these vain pursuits and launched Madison upon that political career for which he displayed so remarkable an aptitude. The organized resistance of the colonies to the mother country and the movement for independence demanded the services of talented young Americans with an interest in political questions. In 1775 James Madison was elected a member of the Orange County Committee, of which his father was chairman. As a member of this body he worked for several months to secure recruits for the army and to insure the effective co-operation of Virginia in the war.[1]

The following year Madison was elected a delegate to the convention which drafted the original constitution of Virginia, including the famous declaration of rights which has been incorporated in all subsequent constitutions of that State. This declaration was largely the work of George Mason, but Madison procured an important change in it respecting religious freedom, substituting a phraseology which declared freedom of conscience to be a natural right and not merely an object of toleration.[2] This was his only contribution to the new frame of government, but it would scarcely be denied that it was a notable one, particularly in view of the fact that most of the older and more prominent delegates were strongly committed to the idea of state control of religion.[3]

Following the adjournment of the convention Madison was elected to the House of Delegates of the Virginia legislature. Here he met Jefferson for the first time. The ac-

[1] *Autobiography.*

[2] *Ibid.*

[3] Hunt, *Life of Madison*, p. 12.

quaintance ripened into a lasting friendship, based upon mutual admiration and respect and a general harmony of ideas.[1] A year later Madison stood for re-election to the Assembly, but this time defeat was his destiny because of his refusal, as he explained it, to court the favor of the voters "by the corrupting influence of spirituous liquors." His defiance of this time-honored custom was represented as the effect of pride or meanness.[2] He was not destined to be excluded long from public life, however. The very same year the Assembly elected him to membership in the Council of State, a kind of advisory cabinet for the Governor. He served as a member of this body until 1779, when he was appointed a delegate to the Continental Congress.[3]

As a member of the Confederation Congress Madison labored earnestly to secure for the general government more effective means of raising revenue for the conduct of the war. The country was rapidly sinking into bankruptcy. The paper Continental currency stood in the ratio of two hundred dollars to one dollar of specie. The States persisted in paying their quotas, when they paid them at all, in worthless paper, in spite of the efforts of Congress to obtain contributions in produce.[4] Madison made several recommendations in the hope of ameliorating conditions. First of all he proposed that Congress should address a formal recommendation to the States to discontinue their emissions of paper, but this suggestion met with a cool reception and was abandoned. His next proposal was more

[1] *Ibid.*, p. 12.
[2] *Autobiography.*
[3] Hunt, *Life of Madison*, p. 32.
[4] *Ibid.*, p. 35.

extreme, but he believed it would be effective. He advised that the Articles of Confederation be amended to give Congress jurisdiction over the trade and property of States that refused to pay their quotas, so that they might be forced to live up to their obligations. Although Congress was willing to consider such a measure, it was not adopted. Finally he advocated with all his might the adoption of a proposal to empower the general government to levy a duty on imports. In February, 1781, Congress resolved to request from the States the necessary power. Rhode Island flatly refused; some others protested against it or took no action at all. Not until the eve of the Philadelphia Convention could the consent of all thirteen be obtained, and then it was too late.[1]

Article V of the Articles of Confederation provided that no delegate in Congress should hold office for more than three years in any six year period. Madison accordingly returned to private life in June, 1783. A year later, however, he was again elected to the Virginia House of Delegates, where he continued to serve until 1787. Broadened in outlook and experience as compared with his earlier service in this body, he took a hand in almost every phase of legislative activity. He succeeded in defeating a project of the conservatives to impose a general assessment for the support of the Christian religion, and procured the adoption of a measure for completing the disestablishment of the Anglican Church, a movement begun by Jefferson in 1779. He urged a grant to Congress of the power to regulate commerce, and he was largely instrumental in bringing about the series of interstate conferences which

[1] *Ibid.*, pp. 36-43.

led to the Annapolis Convention of 1786, and ultimately to the Philadelphia Convention of 1787.[1]

Madison was now approaching the most significant period of his career. The years were fraught with anxiety and turmoil. In 1786 Shays' Rebellion had frightened the creditor classes and those who loved order as the supreme good. The omnipotent legislatures of the States were enacting stay and tender laws and emitting, or threatening to emit, floods of paper money. Against a background of jealously guarded local sovereignty, the powers of the Confederation were sinking into desuetude. Conservative and moderate leaders throughout the country were coming to the conviction that the general government must be given a more energetic character. The failure of most of the States to send delegates to the Annapolis Convention was seized upon by Hamilton, Madison, and others as a good opportunity for calling a new convention of all the States to revise the Federal system.[2]

After another brief period as a member of the Confederation Congress in the spring of 1787, Madison entered upon his duties as a delegate to the Philadelphia Convention, which met on the eighteenth of May of that year. For weeks before the meeting he prepared himself for the part he was to play by extensive researches into ancient and modern constitutions and political theories.[3] The results of this preparation were clearly evident in his speeches before the Convention. Undoubtedly he was

[1] Julius W. Pratt, "James Madison," *Dictionary of American Biography*, vol. XII, pp. 185-86.

[2] E. B. Greene, *The Foundations of American Nationality*, New York, 1922, pp. 570-85.

[3] *Autobiography*.

the best informed member of that body. William Pierce, a delegate from Georgia, described him as "blending the profound politician with the scholar," and as having the most correct knowledge of affairs of the United States of any man in the Union.[1] There was not a debate in which he did not take part, and always with unvarying brilliance and erudition. But if he had not made a single speech or offered a single motion, still his services in the Convention would have been of inestimable value. For he was the unofficial reporter of its proceedings and debates. Never absent for more than a few minutes of the sessions he took careful notes on everything that was said and done, transcribing and amplifying them later in his room. The task almost killed him, but the results are an invaluable heritage to students of political theory.[2]

From the time of his appointment as a delegate Madison seems to have adopted a nationalist position; not because he favored consolidation of the States into a single sovereignty, but because he regarded the weaknesses of the Confederation as a major evil that must first of all be abolished. His correspondence in the spring of 1787 reveals this position very clearly. In a letter to Jefferson on March 10 he declared his conviction that the central government should be vested with a negative "in all cases whatsoever" on the State legislatures, to guard the national rights and interests from invasion, to restrain the States from thwarting and molesting each other, and to keep them from oppressing their own minorities by "paper money and other unrighteous measures which favor the interest

[1] *American Historical Review*, vol. VII, p. 331.
[2] Hunt, *Life of Madison*, p. 116.

of the majority."[1] Writing to Edmund Randolph on April 8, he outlined a plan for a government of national supremacy "with positive and compleat authority in all cases where uniform measures are necessary." He added, however, that he did not think it expedient to attempt a consolidation into one sovereignty. He would strive instead for a middle ground which would "support a due supremacy of the national authority, and leave in force the local authorities so far as they can be subordinately useful."[2]

In the Convention itself Madison did not deviate from the principles already laid down. In his first speech on May 30 he proclaimed his central idea that a national government ought to be established and not "a federal one among sovereign States."[3] On June 19 he urged the establishment of a government for the Union which would accomplish the following ends: (1) prevent encroachments by the States on the Federal authority and counteract the inevitable centrifugal tendency of confederations; (2) prevent trespasses by the States on each other, including particularly the emission of paper money by debtor States to the detriment of creditor States; (3) preserve the internal tranquillity of the States themselves; and (4) promote good government within the States by providing remedies "against the mutability, injustice, and impotence of their laws."[4]

[1] *Writings* (Hunt ed.), vol. II, pp. 326-27.

[2] *Ibid.*, vol. II, pp. 337-38.

[3] Henry D. Gilpin, editor, *The Papers of James Madison*, Washington, 1840, vol. II, p. 752; hereafter cited as *Writings* (Gilpin ed.).

[4] Max Farrand, *Records of the Federal Convention*, vol. I, pp. 316-17.

Madison did not write the famous Virginia Plan presented to the Convention on May 29, and sometimes credited to him, but its character shows the very definite impress of his influence.[1] Moreover, he approved of its nationalist features: a general government deriving its existence directly from the people; a national legislature with authority to negative State laws, to use force against any State recreant to its obligations to the Union, and to legislate wherever the separate States were not competent, or wherever the "harmony of the United States" might be "interrupted by State legislation."[2]

It should be borne in mind that Madison probably did not mean anything like the degree of national supremacy that some of the expressions referred to above seem to convey. At any rate, that was his contention later in his life. For example, he maintained that the term "national" as used by him in the Convention was intended only to distinguish the new government from that of the Confederation, that it was not meant to express the *extent* of power of the general government, but the mode of its operation, which was to be on individuals and not on States. It did not imply any purpose of abolishing the State sovereignties or establishing a consolidated system.[3]

The adjournment of the Convention in September did not terminate Madison's labors of constitutional reconstruction. The new instrument had to be submitted to the

[1] Max Farrand, *The Framing of the Constitution of the United States*, New Haven, 1930, p. 68.

[2] *Documentary History of the Constitution*, Washington, 1905, vol. V, pp. 415-16.

[3] Letter to Thomas Cooper, Dec. 26, 1826, *Writings* (Hunt ed.), vol. IX, p. 268.

old Congress with the provision that that body should lay it before ratifying conventions in the several States. Opponents of the new system immediately launched a movement to have the Constitution amended in Congress. The full measure of Madison's skill and influence was required to frustrate this movement. He perceived that two constitutions would be the result, one the work of the Convention and the other the work of Congress, and that hopeless confusion would follow.[1]

The opposition movement outside of Congress was even more formidable. It sprang from different sources—the inhabitants of the back-country regions, the small farmers, and the debtor classes, in addition to the Scotch-Irish and some of the Germans of Pennsylvania, who were the friends of weak government.[2] Several bases were alleged for their opposition: the new Constitution involved the annihilation of State sovereignty; it contained no bill of rights; it would augment the power of Northern and Eastern capitalists at the expense of the debt-burdened farmers; the authority of Congress over the regulation of commerce would be used by the dominant commercial interest of the North to the disadvantage of the Southern agricultural interest.[3] In October, 1787, Alexander Hamilton and John Jay began a series of newspaper letters to refute these arguments. Soon afterward they invited Madi-

[1] Edward P. Smith, "The Movement towards a Second Constitutional Convention in 1788," *Essays in the Constitutional History of the United States in the Formative Period*, edited by J. F. Jameson, Boston and New York, 1889, p. 56.

[2] Homer C. Hockett, *Political and Social Growth of the United States, 1592-1852*, New York, 1933, p. 300.

[3] Greene, *op. cit.*, pp. 604-9.

son to co-operate. The result was the so-called *Federalist* papers, generally regarded as one of the most significant contributions to political theory ever made in America.[1] Hamilton wrote a majority of the eighty-five letters, but Madison claimed authorship in whole or in part of twenty-six of them, including some of the most valuable in the lot.[2]

In April, 1788, Madison was elected a delegate to the ratifying convention in Virginia, and by reason of his thorough knowledge and convincing logic immediately became the leader of the advocates of the Constitution in that body. Although in poor health at the time he managed to take some part in nearly every debate. He answered effectively every argument that the opposition leaders, Patrick Henry and George Mason, could raise. More than any other man he deserves credit for the final triumph of ratification. Making use of his intimate knowledge of public sentiment in other States, he successfully rebutted Henry's argument that adoption of the Constitution would mean closing the Mississippi to navigation, and thereby won the votes of a number of the delegates from Kentucky.[3] His vigorous defense of religious freedom for many years was rewarded by support for ratification from the Scotch-Irish and German delegates from the Shenandoah Valley.[4] The final vote, after twenty-three days of bitter contention, was 89 to 79 in favor of adhering to the new frame of government.[5]

[1] Hunt, *Life of Madison*, pp. 139-40.
[2] *Writings* (Hunt ed.), vol. V, p. 55 note.
[3] Pratt, *op. cit.*, p. 187.
[4] Greene, *op. cit.*, pp. 609-10.
[5] Hunt, *Life of Madison*, p. 154.

That Madison would be chosen to fill some position of importance in the new government which he had done so much to establish was doubtless taken for granted by all who recognized his accomplishments. But a conflict developed between his own preferences and the wishes of his friends in the matter. Washington desired him as a member of the Senate, and he agreed to stand for election to that body; but he was defeated through the machinations of Patrick Henry, who held the Virginia legislature at that time in the hollow of his hand.[1] Madison's personal preference was for membership in the House of Representatives, because he anticipated for the popularly-elected branch of Congress the dominant position in the Federal government, a position analogous to that of the British House of Commons.[2] In February, 1789, he was elected to the place of his choice.[3]

As a member of the House of Representatives from 1789 until 1797 Madison did some of the noblest work of his whole career. He sponsored the movement for amendments to the Constitution to constitute a bill of rights, with all of the familiar guaranties of personal liberty and protection of property that were ultimately adopted.[4] But doubtless his most valuable service was leadership of the forces in opposition to "high-toned Federalism." No member of the Philadelphia Convention had more assiduously championed the rights of property against the assaults of the masses, yet in the First Congress Madison became

[1] *Ibid.*, p. 162.

[2] *Federalist*, No. 63; Henry Jones Ford, *The Rise and Growth of American Politics*, New York, 1908, pp. 192-93.

[3] Hunt, *Life of Madison*, p. 165.

[4] *Annals of Congress*, vol. I, pp. 433-36.

a relentless opponent of most of Hamilton's fiscal policies. The inconsistency is perhaps more apparent than real. In his defenses of property rights Madison had never contemplated the active encouragement of an aggressive, stock-jobbing capitalism like that involved in the Hamiltonian schemes.[1] The whole tenor of his writings indicates that his conception of property resembled that of Locke; that is, it meant property in the sense of real wealth only, such as land, money, and buildings. It did not embrace "value" created by speculation. He viewed with abhorrence the creation of a huge public debt as injurious to the interests of the people and baneful to the virtue of the government.[2]

In the light of these principles it is not particularly surprising that Madison should have condemned Hamilton's policies for the funding of the national debt, the assumption of the debts of the States, and the establishment of a United States Bank. All of them would redound primarily to the advantage of the Northern moneyed interest. Massachusetts alone, for example, received more in interest on the public debt than did all the Southern States combined.[3] But worst of all, payment of the face value of the certificates of public indebtedness to the existing holders, as Hamilton proposed in his funding scheme, would be grossly unjust. Instead of safeguarding property rights it would defraud the original holders of property justly acquired. It would benefit a class of speculators

[1] Charles A. Beard, *The Economic Origins of Jeffersonian Democracy*, New York, 1915, pp. 51-52.

[2] "The Union," *National Gazette*, April 2, 1792; reprinted in *Writings* (Hunt ed.), vol. VI, p. 105.

[3] Beard, *op. cit.*, p. 393.

who had bought the certificates at a fraction of their face value for no other purpose but to enrich themselves. Madison proposed a compromise under which the current holders would be paid the highest price for their securities that had ever prevailed in the market, the difference between this price and the face value to be paid to the original holders. The proposal was rejected.[1]

After eight years in Congress, ending March 4, 1797, Madison declined re-election and returned to the serenity of private life. But he was not permitted to enjoy it long. The country was again in the throes of crisis. The Revolution in France and the outbreak of war between France and England produced a difficult situation in the United States. Both countries committed breaches of American neutral rights. Appalled by the excesses of the Revolution in France, the Federalists generally sympathized with England. The Republicans, incorrigibly anti-British, were zealous partisans of France. As Republican attacks upon the administration increased, the Federalists retaliated by the enactment of the Alien and Sedition laws. The second of these laws, prescribing fines and prison terms for persons who wrote or uttered defamatory statements against the President or Congress, or sought to bring them into contempt or disrepute, was especially obnoxious to the Republicans, since it was aimed primarily at them. Indictments under the act were numerous, and there were ten convictions with drastic penalties. Republican leaders now felt that some effective measures must be taken to combat these expressions of Federalist arrogance. Accordingly Jefferson and Madison drew up sets of resolutions, which were introduced into the legislatures of

[1] *Annals of Congress*, vol. II, pp. 1193-94.

Kentucky and Virginia, respectively, condemning the Alien and Sedition Acts, and calling upon the other States to concur in the condemnations and to co-operate in maintaining their rights. "It was probably the expectation of the authors that these appeals would draw out similar resolutions in many States and create such pressure upon Congress that it would promptly repeal the laws."[1] No such response was forthcoming, but the Resolutions probably served to intensify discontent with Federalist rule and to insure thereby a Republican triumph in the elections of 1800.

In 1799 Madison accepted election to the Virginia House of Delegates with a view to further opposition to the unconstitutional policies of the Federal government. In the same year of his election he drafted and secured the adoption of the famous Report on the Virginia Resolutions, a long and elaborate statement of his constitutional theories.[2] Two years later, when Jefferson became President, he appointed Madison Secretary of State. The latter's activities in this capacity are of little significance for the development of his political philosophy. In general he merely reflected the will of his chief, not because of servility or lack of imagination, but because the ideas of the two men, regarding foreign affairs at least, were essentially in harmony. After retiring from the Presidency, Jefferson wrote, referring to Madison, "Our principles were the same, and we never differed sensibly in the application of them."[3]

[1] Hockett, *op. cit.*, pp. 349-50.

[2] *Autobiography*.

[3] Letter to Wilson Cary Nicholas, May 25, 1809, *The Writings of Thomas Jefferson* (Ford ed.), New York, 1896, vol. IX, p. 252.

The best part of Madison's career had now come to a close. The sun of his glory had set with his entrance into executive office. In 1808 he was elected President of the United States, largely because of Jefferson's influence, but he added nothing to his reputation in that office; indeed, he rather detracted from it. His record as chief executive was one of treason to his own ideals, of humiliation and failure. It must be conceded, however, that most of his difficulties were bequests from his predecessor. He inherited, first of all, the dispute over West Florida, and his settlement of it was hardly to his credit. He accepted the contention, originally developed by Monroe and Livingston at the time of the Louisiana Purchase, that the Louisiana Territory included West Florida, and that therefore the area in dispute had been sold to the United States in 1803.[1] But there was not a scintilla of evidence for this. The records of the State Department proved that West Florida had not been ceded by Spain to France along with Louisiana in 1800, and consequently could not have been sold to the United States by the French three years later.[2] Even Napoleon himself finally advised the American government that it did not have the shadow of a claim to support its contentions.[3] But these considerations did not deter Madison. He was convinced that West Florida "was essential to our interests."[4] In the summer of 1810 a revolution, engineered by Americans, broke out in the province.

[1] Henry Adams, *History of the United States during the Administrations of Jefferson and Madison*, New York, 1889, vol. II, pp. 70-72.

[2] *Ibid.*, vol. III, p. 56.

[3] Julius W. Pratt, *The Expansionists of 1812*, New York, 1925, p. 70.

[4] *Writings* (Hunt ed.), vol. VII, p. 192.

A declaration of independence was issued, followed by a request for annexation to the United States. Soon afterward Madison issued a proclamation taking formal possession of the disputed territory,[1] thereby completing what has been called "the most disgraceful diplomatic transaction of our history."[2]

The gravest of all the problems confronting Madison as President was the violation of American neutral rights by Great Britain and France. And the record of the administration in dealing with this problem was not much more creditable than in the case of West Florida. Since 1803 England and France had been engaged in a desperate struggle for domination of the European continent. As the possibility of a military triumph for either side became more remote, both belligerents resorted to commercial weapons. In their attempts to blockade each other's coasts they found it necessary to interfere with neutral shipping. Jefferson had sought to bring the offenders to account by an embargo policy, but at the end of his administration the Embargo Act was repealed. At the beginning of Madison's term a Non-Intercourse Act was substituted, permitting commerce with all nations except France and England, and authorizing the President to revive trade with either of these countries upon revocation of its restrictions against American ships.[3] This gave the wily Napoleon his opportunity for a little chicane. In 1810 he tricked Madison into believing that the French restrictive acts, the Berlin and Milan Decrees, were in process

[1] Henry Adams, *op. cit.*, vol. V, p. 306.

[2] I. J. Cox, "The American Intervention in West Florida," *American Historical Review*, vol. XVII (1911-12), p. 311.

[3] Hockett, *op. cit.*, p. 388.

of being revoked. As the weeks lengthened into months Madison began to realize that he had been duped. But he concealed his misgivings and tried to save the situation by forcing Great Britain into a repeal of her Orders in Council, which were designed to shut out American trade with France.[1] It was a fatal policy, almost certain to lead to war.

These were not the only causes that imbued Madison and his party with the martial spirit. From various sources subtle influences were exerting their deadly effect. James Monroe, appointed Secretary of State in April, 1811, came into office with the firm conviction that war was the only proper recourse. This opinion he kept dinning into the President's ears day and night.[2] The election of 1810 resulted in the choice of a surprisingly large number of Republicans who openly avowed their desire for war. Madison was evidently impressed, for almost immediately he assumed a more belligerent attitude toward Great Britain.[3] But probably the most potent of all the influences was the growth of sentiment in the South and West that war would be a justifiable means of extending the American empire—of eliminating British influence over the Indians on the frontier, and making possible the conquest of Canada and Florida.[4] This was the sentiment represented in Congress in 1811-1812 by the so-called War Hawks. They were not primarily interested in taking up arms for a redress of

[1] Charles C. Tansill, "Robert Smith, Secretary of State," *The American Secretaries of State and Their Diplomacy*, edited by Samuel F. Bemis, New York, 1927, vol. III, p. 181.

[2] Edward Channing, *A History of the United States*, New York, 1912, vol. IV, p. 450.

[3] Hockett, *op. cit.*, p. 392.

[4] Pratt, *The Expansionists of 1812*, pp. 12-13.

commercial grievances; their paramount object was the extension of the agrarian interest.[1]

It is a mistake, however, to suppose that a group of rabid swashbucklers in Congress drove a reluctant administration into the War of 1812. The stimulus to armed conflict came equally from Congress and the administration.[2] There is plenty of evidence that the President and his Secretary of State had been contemplating the possibility of military action for some time. In his message to Congress in November, 1811, Madison recommended some rather extensive preparations for war.[3] In the same year he purchased the famous Henry Letters and transmitted them to Congress in March, 1812, in the hope of convicting Great Britain, as well as certain Federalists, of plots to dismember the United States.[4]

On June 1, 1812, Madison transmitted his war message to Congress. He reviewed the various grievances of the United States against Great Britain, charging His Majesty's government with plundering our commerce, cutting off the legitimate markets for our staples, and aiming destructive blows at our agricultural and maritime interests. He accused British agents of fomenting hostility among the Indians on our frontier, and encouraging savage warfare against our settlements. He called upon Congress to decide whether the United States should continue passive under the accumulation of wrongs or "oppose force to force in defense of their national rights." He was "happy in the

[1] Charles A. and Mary R. Beard, *The Rise of American Civilization*, New York, 1930, vol. I, p. 393.

[2] Channing, *op. cit.*, vol. IV, p. 454.

[3] James D. Richardson, *Messages and Papers of the Presidents*, Washington, 1896, vol. I, p. 491.

[4] *American State Papers, Documents Legislative and Executive*, Washington, 1832, vol. III, p. 545.

assurance that the decision will be worthy the enlightened and patriotic councils of a virtuous, a free, and a powerful nation."[1] In other words he knew very well that the decision would be for war. On the eighteenth of the same month war was formally declared.[2]

That there was no adequate justification for an armed clash with Great Britain in 1812 seems to be the judgment of most competent historians. Most of the earlier grievances had by that time been removed. The British government had modified the Orders in Council, with the promise of further modifications, and had made some recompense for the attack on the *Chesapeake*, a public vessel of the United States.[3] The evil of impressments, the principal remaining grievance and the chief reason for war alleged by Madison, appears to have been grossly exaggerated. The Massachusetts legislature conducted an inquiry into the subject in 1812 and found amazing duplications in the list of 6057 cases reported to Congress by the President. In the course of the inquiry the largest ship-owner in New England, a Republican withal, testified that he could remember only two cases of impressment from his vessels in the past two years out of an average of three hundred seamen employed annually.[4] It is perhaps significant that after negotiations to end the war had begun, Madison himself suggested that the American commissioners drop the demand for the abandonment of impressments.[5]

On March 4, 1817, Madison retired from the Presi-

[1] *American State Papers, Foreign Relations*, vol. III, pp. 405-7.
[2] Channing, *op. cit.*, vol. IV, p. 452.
[3] Henry Adams, *op. cit.*, vol. VI, p. 225.
[4] Channing, *op. cit.*, vol. IV, pp. 481-82.
[5] Pratt, "James Madison," *Dictionary of American Biography*, vol. XII, p. 192.

dency after eight stormy years occupied principally by foreign troubles. During the remainder of his life he accepted few public employments. In 1829 he was elected a delegate to the Virginia constitutional convention, but he made only one speech, in which he proposed a compromise between opposing factions on the suffrage. He declared in his *Autobiography*, written some time afterward, that his own preference would have been universal manhood suffrage, or as close to that as possible. Probably a freehold suffrage, like that desired by Jefferson, was what he really had in mind. His chief interest after leaving the Presidency was the University of Virginia, in the founding of which he had been the faithful assistant of Jefferson.[1] He served on the board of visitors of the institution until Jefferson's death in 1826, when he succeeded him as rector.[2] In his last years Madison devoted much time to correspondence in defense of the constitutional system in what he believed to be its original purity, based on the principle of divided sovereignty. He attacked vigorously the cardinal heresies of that time—the doctrines of nullification and secession on the one hand, and the theory of absolute national sovereignty on the other. On June 28, 1836, he died peacefully in his chair in the eighty-sixth year of his age.[3]

The genius of Madison is not fully revealed by an account of his public activities. In the intervals between his public employments, and sometimes in the midst of them, he found time for a great variety of pursuits, chiefly scientific and philosophical. A letter which he wrote to Jefferson

[1] Hunt, *Life of Madison*, p. 368.
[2] *Ibid.*, p. 368.
[3] *Ibid.*, p. 384.

in 1784 illustrates pretty well the breadth of his interests. He asked his friend to procure for him in Paris French translations of the historians of the Roman Empire during its decline, Pascal's *Provincial Letters*, additional volumes of Buffon as they should be published, and volumes by French writers on the economics of different nations.[1] The work of Buffon, the French natural historian, interested Madison profoundly, and he made extensive researches of his own into the same subject. By careful study, measurement, and comparison of internal and external structures of various animal species he sought to test some of the Frenchman's famous theories.[2]

As a scientist and philosopher Madison was in many ways a true representative of the eighteenth century—in the diffusion of his interests, in his naïve assumption of a universal competence, but above all, in his acceptance of the dogma of a mechanistic universe controlled throughout by immutable law. Among his papers was found an unfinished essay entitled, "The Symmetry of Nature," in which he attempted to show the harmony of the physical world and the life of man under the controlling power of kindred laws.[3] In regard to religion also, Madison's beliefs conformed to the usual eighteenth century pattern. Like Jefferson he professed a kind of "natural religion" not far removed from deism. He referred to belief in a God as "essential to the moral order of the world and to the happiness of man,"[4] but he considered the acceptance of any brand

[1] *Writings* (Hunt ed.), vol. II, pp. 133-34.

[2] Hunt, *Life of Madison*, pp. 96-97.

[3] *Ibid.*, pp. 101-2.

[4] Letter to Frederick Beasley, Nov. 20, 1825, *Writings* (Hunt ed.), vol. IX, p. 230.

of Christian orthodoxy intellectually impossible.[1] Only in his refusal to idealize the "natural" life of the "noble savage," and in his denial of the inherent goodness of man, did he part company on general questions with the *philosophes* of the Age of Reason. He believed that the condition of the red men should be improved by substituting "the comforts and habits of civilized life for the torpid indolence of the wigwam."[2] At times his observations in the realm of social theory showed flashes of genius, particularly when he anticipated Malthus by explaining the prevalence of poverty as due to the pressure of population on the means of subsistence.[3]

If Plato had lived in America about 1800, he might have chosen Madison as one example of the philosopher-kings who should rule the Republic. And the choice would not have been so inappropriate. Madison was a true aristocrat in many ways, who regarded governing as the most honorable of professions, a profession requiring the most thorough knowledge of political science and the deepest instincts of devotion to public life. He adhered to an impeccable code of political morality. Although often in straitened circumstances he consistently refused to regard public office as a source of private gain.[4] While a member of Congress he declined to accept articles of stationery provided at government expense.[5] Throughout his political

[1] Notes of Speech against Religious Assessments, *Writings* (Hunt ed.), vol. II, pp. 88-89.

[2] Letter to Rev. Jedidiah Morse, Feb. 26, 1822, manuscript, Princeton University Library.

[3] Letter to Jefferson, June 19, 1786, *Writings* (Hunt ed.), vol. II, pp. 247-48.

[4] Sidney Howard Gay, *James Madison*, Boston, 1892, pp. 25-26.

[5] *Autobiography*.

career he resolved never to deal in public property—land, debts, or money.[1] He was one of the few prominent members of the Constitutional Convention who did not own public securities.[2] He disapproved the practice of legislative bodies in raising the wages of their own members, and he refused such an increase voted by the legislature of Virginia.[3]

Madison's true greatness lay, of course, in his contributions to the theory of the state and of the American Constitution. To show something of the nature and influence of these contributions is the purpose of the pages that follow.

[1] *Ibid.*

[2] Charles A. Beard, *An Economic Interpretation of the Constitution of the United States*, New York, 1925, p. 125.

[3] *Autobiography.*

TWO

# General Theory of the State

## THE FOUNDATION OF THE STATE AND THE BASIS OF POLITICS

TO the men of Madison's day the conception of the state as an organism, as a product of evolution, was almost unknown. With the fewest of exceptions they regarded the state as artificial and founded on agreement. In similar fashion they thought of sovereignty as alienable and divisible, and law as dependent upon consent for its validity.[1] James Wilson in one of his famous lectures had summarized the prevailing views about as neatly as anyone could desire: "The only reason why a free and independent man was ever bound by the laws was this—that he bound himself. If one free and independent man, an original sovereign, may do all this, why may not an aggregate of free and independent men, a collection of original sovereigns, do likewise?"[2] Not until the publication of John C. Calhoun's *Disquisition on Government* in 1851 was there any definite affirmation in America of the opposing theory that the state is organic, and that life subject to its authority is the natural and necessary condition of man, and not the result of his deliberate choice.

[1] A. C. McLaughlin, *The Courts, the Constitution and Parties,* Chicago, 1912, p. 196.

[2] *Works* (Andrews ed.), vol. II, p. 153; quoted by A. C. McLaughlin, *The Foundations of American Constitutionalism,* New York, 1932, p. 84.

Throughout his long career Madison never questioned the compact theory of the foundation of the state. To a large extent it was the core of his whole philosophy. As late as 1830 when theories of artificial creation by agreement of a political society out of a state of nature had been pretty generally abandoned in Europe, Madison declared that the idea of a compact, express or implied, "is a fundamental principle of free government."[1] He admitted that the compact is only theoretical in most cases, but he insisted that it is possible for it to be realized in unoccupied territory.[2] At times he appeared to believe in a duality of compacts, the first a social compact by which a civil society is formed, and the second a political compact by which that society establishes a government, or a "sovereign." When the Revolution dissolved the ties that bound the colonies to Great Britain, for example, "the colonies remained as a political society." They did not revert to a state of nature. The social compact was not dissolved, but merely the political compact which bound the people in allegiance to a sovereign, the British government. Once this compact had been terminated the people of the colonies were free to enter into a new political compact to set up a government over them.[3]

The political compact, however, was almost exclusively the subject of Madison's concern. He was little interested in a hypothetical state of nature where man would be supposed to live under a condition of anarchy. His political philosophy began at the point where man, "because of his weakness and wants," contracted with his fellow-men to

[1] Letter to N. P. Trist, *Writings* (Hunt ed.), vol. IX, p. 355 note.

[2] Manuscript, *Madison Papers*, Library of Congress.

[3] *Annals of Congress*, vol. I, pp. 405-6.

form "an association of individuals under a common authority, whereby each may have the protection of the whole against danger from without, and enjoy in safety within, the advantages of social intercourse and an exchange of the necessaries and comforts of life."[1] It is to be noted that the political compact is never under any circumstances an agreement between subjects and governors; the government is not a party to the compact, but a creature of it; the parties are the governed exclusively. Moreover, the compact is assumed to be permanent unless otherwise expressed. The government is not permanent but alterable by the authority which created it.[2]

Why is the political compact, establishing government, entered into? A suggestion of the reason has been given in the preceding paragraph. A complete answer can be obtained only through an extended analysis of Madison's theories on the basis of politics and the purpose of government. Human beings, he maintained, are generally governed by rather base and selfish motives, by suspicion, jealousy, desire for aggrandizement, and disinclination to do more than is required by convenience or self-interest, or exacted of them by force.[3] But worse than the motives themselves are the results, particularly the tendency of men to unite into factions for the attainment of some particular advantage inimical to the general good. The latent causes of faction are sown in the nature of man himself, in a kind of innate and perverse tendency to fall into jealousy and

[1] Origin of the Constitutional Convention, *Writings* (Hunt ed.), vol. II, p. 391.

[2] Manuscript, *Madison Papers*, Library of Congress.

[3] Jonathan Elliot, *Debates in the Constitutional Conventions*, Washington, 1838, vol. II, p. 199.

rivalry and contention. The love of disputation over religious and political theories and practices, together with herd instincts that lead men to attach themselves to ambitious leaders and adventurers, "have divided mankind into parties, inflamed them with mutual animosities, and rendered them much more disposed to vex and oppress each other than to co-operate for the common good." Indeed this tendency is so strong that where no substantial basis for antagonism exists, "the most frivolous and fanciful distinctions" may be sufficient to plague men into violent hatred and conflict. "But the most common and durable source of faction has been the various and unequal distribution of property." The propertied and the propertyless, the creditors and the debtors, the landed interest, the industrial interest, the commercial interest, the financial interest have always formed distinct elements in society, and the existence of any or all of these elements inevitably results in the growth of factions to advance their interests through political channels.[1] Where overmastering self-interests like these are involved, neither religious nor moral scruples can be depended upon to hold them in check. The establishment of government becomes necessary as the only alternative.[2]

Contrary to the usual opinion Madison did not always look at mankind with such a jaundiced eye. He did not really believe in the *total* depravity of man's political nature. Writing in the *National Gazette* in 1792, he referred to the two conflicting views of human nature out of which opposing political parties commonly develop. According to one view the masses of men are slavish, licentious, ignorant, greedy, and incapable of discerning their true interests,

[1] *Federalist* (Lodge ed.), New York, 1888, No. 10, pp. 53-54.
[2] *Ibid.*, No. 10, p. 56.

much less the interests of the whole people. This theory is the basis of the aristocratic, or anti-republican, parties. On the other hand, there is the theory of the democratic or republican element, according to which the generality of mankind have at least sufficient wisdom and patriotism to be reasonably capable of self-government. Through enlightenment and awakening of their nobler instincts they may be made more so.[1] It is sufficient to observe that Madison was already an active leader of the forces in opposition to Hamilton's policies, so that it is evident he meant to espouse the second of these theories. But even in the Virginia ratifying convention four years earlier, when he found it necessary to justify the cynical views of human nature implicit in the Constitution, he had avowed his allegiance to "the great republican principle that the people have the virtue and the intelligence to select men of virtue and wisdom" for public office. And he deprecated as "a chimerical idea" the belief that mere checks and balances, or any other design of government, could render liberty secure without any assumption of popular virtue.[2] Perhaps the following statement in *Federalist* Number 55, which Madison claimed to have written,[3] embodies pretty well the essence of his view of the human species: "As there is a degree of depravity in mankind which requires a certain degree of circumspection and distrust, so there are other qualities in human nature which justify a certain portion of esteem and confidence."[4]

Even this melioristic view of man's political character

[1] *Writings* (Hunt ed.), vol. VI, pp. 115-18.
[2] Elliot, *op. cit.*, vol. II, p. 393.
[3] *Writings* (Hunt ed.), vol. V, p. 55 note.
[4] Lodge edition, p. 350.

was a far cry from a belief in the inherent goodness of human beings. And the purpose of government in Madison's theory still remained the correction of the evil propensities of man's nature. The most serious of all these is the tendency to invade the property rights of others. Every man, he maintained, has a natural right to acquire property, and he concluded from this that the prime object of government is to protect those faculties from which that right originates.[1] The principal task of modern legislation, as he saw it, is to regulate the various and conflicting economic interests.[2] "Government is instituted to protect property of every sort. This being the end of government, that alone is a just government which impartially secures to every man whatever is his own."[3] Madison sometimes attempted a broader definition of "property" than that which would include merely external possessions. He tried to give the term something of the Lockian connotation of "life, liberty, and estate"; that is to say, man has property in his political and religious opinions, in the liberty and safety of his person, in the free use of his faculties and free choice of the objects on which to employ them.[4] Most of the time, however, he seems to have intended a more restricted meaning for the term, especially during the Constitutional Convention and the period of the ratification controversy, when the "levelling" ambitions of various malcontents were still uppermost in his mind. But as noted in the preceding chapter, even this restricted

[1] *Federalist* (Lodge ed.), No. 10, p. 56.

[2] *Ibid.*, p. 57.

[3] "Property," *National Gazette*, March 29, 1792; reprinted in *Writings* (Hunt ed.), vol. VI, p. 101.

[4] *Ibid.*, vol. VI, pp. 101-2.

meaning did not embrace "paper wealth" created by speculation.[1]

Madison's doctrine of sovereignty rested squarely upon the compact theory of the state. Since all free governments are formed by agreement, the conclusion is unavoidable that sovereignty can be alienated or divided. His reasoning on this subject is fairly consistent. Before the formation of the political compact sovereignty inheres in each individual or group of individuals that is to become a party to it. Who can deny that these have the right to allocate their sovereign powers as they see fit? Moreover, this allocation can be made by the majority; unanimous agreement is not required. For the compact theory supposes "either that it was a part of the original compact, that the will of the majority was to be deemed the will of the whole, or that this was a law of nature, resulting from the nature of political society itself, the offspring of the natural wants of man."[2] But whatever the origin of the law of majority rule, it is evident that it operates as a plenary substitute for the will of the whole society, and that the majority can do anything that could be rightfully done by the concurrence of all the members. That is, the majority, acting for all the parties, can surrender wholly or in part any element of sovereignty except those natural rights which every man reserves to himself when the original compact is formed.[3] Madison had no use for the Blackstonian idea that sovereignty is by its very nature absolute, indivisible, and inalienable. On the contrary he saw what he believed to be the elemental fact of sovereign power as the original

[1] *Supra*, pp. 16-17.

[2] "Sovereignty," *Writings* (Hunt ed.), vol. IX, p. 570.

[3] *Ibid.*, p. 571.

possession of the parties to the political compact. They, or the majority acting for them, could make any disposition of it they thought proper, retaining all of it or surrendering all of it, or retaining part and surrendering the remainder. This conception of sovereignty is fundamental to an understanding of Madison's theory of the nature of the Union, as we shall see in a succeeding chapter.

Such a theory of sovereignty clearly implied a doctrine of the right of revolution, which Madison always adhered to as an ultimate remedy in extreme cases of governmental tyranny or failure to provide for the country's needs. In Number 43 of the *Federalist* he attempted to justify the revolutionary action of the Philadelphia Convention in discarding the Articles of Confederation and providing for a new system of government, by referring to "the transcendent law of nature and of nature's God, which declares that the safety and happiness of society are the objects at which all political institutions aim, and to which all institutions must be sacrificed."[1] In an earlier essay of the same series he was even more explicit. He appealed to the "transcendent and precious right of the people to alter or abolish their governments as to them shall seem most likely to effect their safety and happiness."[2] He virtually denied this right to the people of the several States of the Union, however, so far as their own governments were concerned. In *Federalist* 43 he defended the provision of the Constitution which authorizes Congress "to guarantee to every State in the Union a *republican* form of government." It is certainly conceivable, however, that

[1] Lodge edition, p. 276.

[2] *Ibid.*, No. 40, p. 246.

a majority of the people in a State might decide that their safety and happiness could be effected by a pure democracy, or even by a limited monarchy. But such a conclusion, according to Madison's theory, would have to yield to the superior interest of the other members of the Union in having the form of government under which the compact was entered into substantially maintained.[1]

### THEORY OF THE BEST STATE

Madison had rather definite opinions regarding what would constitute the best state, and it is not difficult to reconstruct his ideal. In the first place, it would be a political society founded upon an agrarian basis, although with sufficient admixtures of other economic activities to eliminate too great a dependence upon foreign countries. But Madison shared with Jefferson a deep and abiding distrust of great cities with their parasitic capitalists and ignorant, exploited mobs. Neither in his judgment had the civic consciousness or impartiality requisite for the highest type of citizenship. In an article in the *National Gazette* for March 8, 1792, he averred that it is not the rural population that furnishes denizens for the Bridewells and Bedlams. These citadels of wretchedness are populated from the distresses and vice of congested cities. The class of citizens who provide for their own needs of food, clothing, and shelter may be regarded as the most truly independent and happy. "They are more: they are the best basis of public liberty, and the strongest bulwark of public safety. It follows that the greater the proportion of this class to the whole society, the more free, the more independent, and the more happy

[1] Lodge edition, p. 270.

must be the society itself."[1] Closely akin to this insistence upon an agrarian basis was his emphasis upon a substantially even distribution of wealth. Measures should be enacted which, without violating the rights of property, would "reduce extreme wealth towards a state of mediocrity, and raise extreme indigence towards a state of comfort."[2]

In the second place, the ideal state must be a republic, as distinguished from a monarchy or a pure democracy. In other words, it must have a form of government based upon representation and extending over a considerable area.[3] In addition it must derive its powers, directly or indirectly, from the great body of society, not from any small proportion or favored class of it; and it must be administered by persons holding their offices during pleasure, for a limited period, or during good behavior.[4] One of the worst forms of government is a pure democracy, that is, one in which the citizens enact and administer the laws directly. Such a government is helpless against the mischiefs of faction. A common passion or interest will almost invariably unite and dominate a majority of the whole, and the form of government itself will facilitate concerted action among that majority to impose its will upon the rest. "Hence it is that such democracies have ever been spectacles of turbulence and contention; have ever been found incompatible with personal security or the rights of property; have in gen-

[1] "Republican Distribution of Citizens"; reprinted in *Writings* (Hunt ed.), vol. VI, pp. 97-99.

[2] "Parties," *National Gazette*, Jan. 23, 1792; reprinted in *Writings* (Hunt ed.), vol. VI, p. 86.

[3] *Federalist* (Lodge ed.), No. 10, p. 57.

[4] *Ibid.*, No. 39, p. 233.

eral been as short in their lives as they have been violent in their deaths."[1] There are two obvious remedies against this. One is to provide for a system of representation, so as to "refine and enlarge the public views by passing them through the medium of a chosen body of citizens, whose wisdom may best discern the true interest of their country, and whose patriotism and love of justice will be least likely to sacrifice it to temporary and partial considerations."[2]

Such an arrangement may well mean that the popular will, expressed by these representatives, will be more in harmony with the good of the whole than if expressed directly by the people themselves. But representative government alone is not sufficient. Human beings are not to be trusted with unlimited opportunities for the abuse of power. Besides, it is not certain that the representatives will aways constitute an elite devoted to justice and the public good. Men of factious tempers and malevolent designs may occasionally win elections and then betray the interest of the people. The most effectual safeguard against this evil is to enlarge the sphere of government, to make the area and population of the republic extensive enough so that the society will naturally divide itself into a great number of diverse interests and groups. And the greater the number and variety of these, the more nearly impossible it will be for any faction or combination of them, with a common purpose, to constitute a majority. Furthermore, the greater the number of diverse elements, the more difficult will it be for ambitious leaders to discern the purposes which animate them, and the greater will be the risk of inviting any of them into a proposed combination. Mutual distrust

[1] *Ibid.*, No. 10, p. 59.
[2] *Ibid.*, No. 10, pp. 59-60.

based upon ignorance of each other's motives will tend to keep the several factions isolated.[1] It was the old policy of Divide and Rule dedicated to a more creditable purpose than that usually associated with the maxim.

Madison regarded government by faction as the besetting sin of modern states. He defined a faction as "a number of citizens, whether amounting to a majority or a minority of the whole, who are united and actuated by some common impulse of passion, or of interest, adverse to the rights of other citizens or to the permanent and aggregate interests of the community."[2] Government by faction is to be condemned since it permits the same men to be parties and judges in their own cause. In a controversy between creditors and debtors, both are parties, and neither should have the right to impose its will upon the other. "Justice ought to hold the balance between them." In like manner any question involving the mercantile or manufacturing or landed interest, or the apportionment of taxes, should not be decided at the behest of a powerful faction concerned with its own aggrandizement, but by legislators acting with an exact impartiality, and with a sole regard for justice and the public welfare.[3] Thus Madison recognized the class conflict as the basis of politics, but he refused to regard a class dictatorship as either necessary or desirable. Whether he actually believed that legislators would ever be selected who would mediate between conflicting interests with an exact impartiality and regard for the public welfare is not possible to determine, but he evi-

def of faction

NB

[1] *Federalist* (Lodge ed.), No. 10, pp. 58-60; Farrand, *Records of the Federal Convention*, vol. I, pp. 134-36.

[2] *Federalist* (Lodge ed.), No. 10, p. 52.

[3] *Ibid.*, No. 10, p. 55.

dently entertained few illusions in the matter as is evidenced by his earnest attention to plans for preventing rule by one or more factions.

Not only must the government of the ideal state be organized on republican principles; it must embody a federal system as well. Madison declared the latter to be "essential to the complete success of republicanism in any form."[1] He thought the government of the United States, combining as it does the principles of both republicanism and federalism, "the best legacy ever left by law-givers to their country, and the best lesson ever given to the world by its benefactors."[2] A consolidated or unitary government, particularly in a country with a diversity of interests, could not but foster tyranny and pave "the highroad to monarchy." The inability of one legislature to accommodate all the various objects of so great a sphere of government would inevitably force a transfer of many of them to the executive department. The splendor and the number of the prerogatives of the latter would open the way for despotism. Ambitious men, tempted by the magnitude of executive power, would corrupt or pervert the elective system, and hereditary dictatorship would be the result. The process would be abetted by the inability of the people to understand or control the complexity of things. Discouraged and helpless they would abdicate their proper functions and welcome Caesarism as the only refuge.[3]

[1] Letter to Robert E. Lee, Feb. 22, 1830, *Letters and Other Writings of James Madison*, published by order of Congress, Philadelphia, 1865; hereafter cited as *Writings* (Cong. ed.).

[2] "The Government of the United States," *National Gazette*, Feb. 6, 1792; reprinted in *Writings* (Hunt ed.), vol. VI, p. 91.

[3] "Consolidation," *National Gazette*, Dec. 5, 1791; reprinted in *Writings* (Hunt ed.), vol. VI, p. 67.

However, decentralization must not be carried to the point of establishing a confederacy, with the local units the sole repositories of effective sovereignty. True federalism implies a division of sovereignty between the local governments and the general government, with the people the subjects of both. The vices inherent in confederacies are of such magnitude as to make that form of government productive of nothing but anarchy and confusion. Every league or confederation from the Amphictyonic League to the Dutch Republic which has depended upon independent sovereignties for its existence has had a record of misgovernment, particularistic jealousy, and insecurity from foreign domination. Only through a just combination of the proper amount of energy in the central government with the proper degree of distribution of powers made by the people themselves can these evils be avoided.[1]

One further check against despotism of any sort is necessary to fulfill the requirements of the best state, and that is the principle of the separation of powers. No matter how the conditions of his political life changed, Madison never modified his conviction of the fundamental value of this principle. In the *Federalist* he declared the accumulation of legislative, executive, and judicial powers in the same hands, whether those of a monarch, an aristocracy, or an elective assembly, worthy of being pronounced "the very definition of tyranny."[2] As a member of the First Congress he proposed an amendment to the Constitution providing that "the Legislative Department shall never exercise the powers vested in the Executive or Judicial, nor the Executive exercise the powers vested in the Legislative or Judicial, nor the Judicial exercise the powers vested in the

[1] Elliot, *Debates*, vol. II, pp. 119-23.

[2] Lodge edition, No. 47, p. 300.

Legislative or Executive Departments."[1] In his Report on the Virginia Resolutions, written in 1799, he affirmed it to be an axiom in the science of government that a separation of the three departments is necessary to the preservation of public liberty.[2] Even as President of the United States in a time of crisis he strove to avoid every appearance of usurping any of the powers of the other branches of the government.[3]

On the other hand, Madison rejected the idea that the separation of powers must always be complete and arbitrary, that there should be no fusion of powers whatever, that the executive, for example, should never be allowed any powers of a legislative character. He demonstrated from an analysis of the British Constitution, Montesquieu's "mirror of political liberty," that the celebrated author of *The Spirit of the Laws* in advocating the separation of powers did not mean that one branch of the government should never have a partial agency in, or control over another branch, but rather that the whole power of one department should never be exercised by the same hands which possessed the whole power of another department.[4] Indeed, according to Madison, unless the several departments are so far connected and blended as to give each a considerable control over the others, the degree of separation which theory requires as essential to a free government can never in practice be really maintained.[5] As a matter of fact Madison was much less of an extremist on the subject than some of his

[1] *Annals of Congress,* vol. I, pp. 435-36.
[2] *Writings* (Hunt ed.), vol. VI, p. 371.
[3] *Infra,* Chapter Five.
[4] *Federalist* (Lodge ed.), No. 47, pp. 301-4.
[5] *Ibid.,* No. 48, p. 319.

contemporaries. In the Federal Convention he argued that association of the judges with the executive in revising the laws would not violate the principle of the separation of powers.[1] By an interesting contrast George Mason objected to the new Constitution partly because it made the Vice President of the United States the presiding officer of the Senate, "thereby dangerously blending the executive and legislative powers."[2]

As another essential Madison considered that any state approaching a perfect form must have a coercive government. In other words, the check and balance scheme must not be carried so far as to destroy the energy of the state. Enough has been said to show Madison's fear of despotism resulting from the concentration of power, but he also feared anarchy and what he was accustomed to call the "imbecility" of government. In Number 37 of the *Federalist* he affirmed that one of the great problems of the Convention had been the perfection of a nice adjustment between the requisite stability and energy in government and the strict attention due to liberty and the republican form.[3] But the essence of government, he maintained, is force. "What is the meaning of government? An institution to make people do their duty. A government leaving it to a man to do his duty or not, as he pleases, would be a new species of government, or rather no government at all."[4] Man is a selfish animal as well as a social being. In some degree his selfishness may be restrained by his social feelings, by his respect for character, by his conscience.

[1] Farrand, *Records of the Federal Convention*, vol. II, p. 77.
[2] *Documentary History of the Constitution*, vol. IV, p. 318.
[3] Lodge edition, p. 217.
[4] Elliot, *Debates*, vol. II, p. 309.

These favorable qualities are all valuable as auxiliaries, but they will not serve as a substitute for the coercive attributes of government and law.[1] The history of all republics justifies the conclusion that if the bonds of the government be relaxed, confusion will ensue. Anarchy is the chief breeding ground of despotism, the very evil that an excess of liberty is supposed to prevent.[2] Madison insisted, however, that the powers of government must operate on individuals, not on political subdivisions of the state. Coercion of the local units by the general government could only result in a state of war between two or more opposing sovereignties.[3]

At one time in his life Madison appeared to turn away from the doctrine of the coercive basis of government. In the Second Congress he condemned the argument in favor of the United States Bank that it would increase the energy and strength of the administration. He maintained that the government of the United States should rely upon "the enlightened opinion and affection of the people" as the only solid basis for its support.[4] This declaration appears to be something of an exception to his general opinion, for, as already indicated, in the Virginia Convention of 1829 he returned to the doctrine he had developed during the debates on the Federal Constitution.[5] Professor Parrington considered Madison's emphasis upon coercive government as marking a fundamental conflict between his philos-

VIP

[1] Speech in Virginia Constitutional Convention of 1829, *Writings* (Hunt ed.), vol. IX, p. 361.

[2] Elliot, *Debates*, vol. II, pp. 295-96.

[3] *Ibid.*, vol. II, p. 200.

[4] *Annals of Congress*, vol. II, p. 1959.

[5] *Supra*, p. 43.

ophy and that of Jefferson.[1] The difference can rather easily be accounted for by reference to Madison's more cynical, and perhaps more realistic, view of human nature.

Finally, according to Madison, no state can be considered of superior excellence that does not possess the quality of stability. "Stability in government is essential to national character and to the advantages annexed to it, as well as to that repose and confidence in the minds of the people, which are among the chief blessings of civil society."[2] An even course of public policy is especially requisite for the security of private rights. "Sudden changes and legislative interferences, in cases of personal rights, become jobs in the hands of enterprising and influential speculators, and snares to the more industrious and less informed part of the community." Measures must be adopted which will banish such unwholesome economic activity and create a favorable environment for the man of prudence and industry.[3] It was for these reasons that Madison condemned *ex post facto* laws, laws impairing the obligation of contracts, and emissions of paper money[4] that is, not in order to give an indiscriminate protection to the rich against the masses, but to preserve a regime of healthy individual enterprise by securing to the farmer, the merchant, and the small manufacturer the just rewards of industry, thrift,

[1] *Main Currents in American Thought*, New York, 1927, vol. I, pp. 285, 345.

[2] *Federalist* (Lodge ed.), No. 37, p. 217.

[3] *Ibid.*, No. 44, p. 279.

[4] Charles Warren avers that Madison's objections to the fiat money emissions and stay and tender laws of the States were derived from his fear that such laws would create dissension within the Union and endanger its existence. *The Making of the Constitution*, Boston, 1929, p. 79.

and useful labor: in other words the very same motives that largely inspired the attack on the Bank and Hamilton's funding and assumption policies. It was partly for these reasons also that he recommended a Senate to curb the fickle tendencies of the representatives of the people. "Every new regulation concerning commerce or revenue, or in any manner affecting the value of the different species of property, presents a new harvest to those who watch the change and can trace its consequences; a harvest reared not by themselves but by the toils and cares of the great body of their fellow-citizens." The effect of public instability is always to benefit "the sagacious, the enterprising, and the moneyed few over the industrious and uninformed mass of the people."[1]

Unlike some of his contemporaries Madison indulged in no Utopian fancies. He did not believe in the infinite perfectibility of man's estate, nor in the omniscience of political philosophers. Consequently he would have admitted that the best state, reconstructed above, falls far short of perfection. "The purest of human blessings," he was wont to say, "must have a portion of alloy in them; the choice must always be made, if not of the lesser evil, at least of the greater, not the perfect, good."[2] The greatest adepts in political science have never been able to solve some of its simplest problems: to discriminate and define, for example, with adequate certainty, the three great provinces of government, the legislative, executive, and judicial; or even to distinguish the privileges and powers of the different branches

[1] *Federalist* (Lodge ed.), No. 42, p. 390; claimed by both Madison and Hamilton, but judging by its content, probably written by the former.

[2] *Ibid.*, No. 41, p. 249.

of the legislature.[1] The vital question, therefore, that must be asked of any proposed constitution is not, Is it perfect? but, Is it better than the one it is designed to replace?[2]

## THE PROVINCE OF GOVERNMENT

Madison's general philosophy of the state may well be taken to embrace his theory of the province of government. As a disciple of Locke, Montesquieu, and Jefferson he naturally did not posit a very extensive sphere within which government could operate. Indeed he took as major premises the *dicta* that "The necessity of any government is a misfortune,"[3] and "Government is the greatest of all reflections on human nature."[4] So far as these assumptions were concerned, he was apparently in perfect agreement with Jefferson that "Government is a necessary evil," and with Paine that "Society springs from our wants, government from our wickedness."

The most concise statement which Madison ever made of his theory of the sphere of government is to be found in his final message to Congress on December 3, 1816. He admonished his countrymen to cherish the following pattern of government as an ideal:

> A government pursuing the public good as its sole object, and regulating its means by the great principles consecrated in its charter, and by those moral principles to which they are so well allied; a government which watches over the purity of elections, the freedom of speech and the press, the trial by jury, and the equal

[1] *Ibid.*, No. 37, p. 219.
[2] *Ibid.*, No. 38, p. 229.
[3] Majority Governments, *Writings* (Hunt ed.), vol. IX, p. 523.
[4] *Federalist* (Lodge ed.), No. 51, p. 323.

> interdict against encroachments and compacts between religion and state; which maintains inviolably the maxims of public faith, the security of persons and property, and encourages in every authorized mode that general diffusion of knowledge which guarantees to public liberty its permanency and to those who possess the blessing the true enjoyment of it; a government which avoids intrusion on the internal repose of other nations and repels them from its own . . . ; a government, in a word, whose conduct within and without may bespeak the most noble of all ambitions—that of promoting peace on earth and good will to men.[1]

In other words, his vision was that of a government whose functions are largely negative, that regards its subjects solely as individuals with independent rights to get as much out of life as their industry, talent, and good luck will permit. It is the duty of the government to protect its subjects in the exercise of these rights, to provide a favorable environment for the development of individual faculties, especially the faculty of acquiring property, and to educate the young for the same blessings. Beyond this point the obligations of the government cease.

Generally speaking, Madison adhered in theory to the *laissez-faire* principles defined in the foregoing message, although with numerous modifications. He had only a limited conception of the state as a positive agency for promoting the public welfare. He did not believe in the omnicompetence of government to effect the prosperity or misery of its subjects. It is rather, he maintained, the mission of

[1] Richardson, *Messages and Papers of the Presidents,* vol. I, p. 580.

government to provide a *milieu* in which every citizen can garner the rewards of his industry, economy, and talent. The supreme *desiderata* for such a society are confidence, justice, and security. These it is the exalted object of government to provide. No country in the world can do without them. They are the supreme inducements to labor, to the creation of wealth; and the chief aids to debtors, for they raise the value of property and furnish relief to the insolvent.[1] It is the function of government also to prohibit monopolies, exemptions, and all other special privileges which interfere with equality of economic opportunity.[2]

Madison did not consider it desirable that government should intervene directly in the interest of the less fortunate members of society. Compassion is due them, he graciously conceded, but not direct beneficence.[3] Moreover, even if such intervention were desirable, the results would not be successful. In the main he envisaged the condition of the lower classes in Malthusian and Ricardian terms, anticipating some of the famous theories of the two great English exponents of the "dismal science." He was apprehensive that a certain degree of poverty would always be inseparable from congestion of population. No matter how wisely property may be distributed, there will inevitably develop a surplus of inhabitants who can no longer be occupied in ministering to the essential needs of each other.[4] He was skeptical of all plans to improve the condi-

[1] Elliot, *Debates*, vol. II, p. 394.

[2] "Property," *National Gazette*, March 29, 1792; reprinted in *Writings* (Hunt ed.), vol. VI, p. 102.

[3] Elliot, *Debates*, vol. II, p. 394.

[4] Letter to Jefferson, June 19, 1786, *Writings* (Hunt ed.), vol. II, pp. 247-48.

tion of the masses because of this persistent tendency to increase their own numbers with every amelioration of their economic status. The increase in numbers can lead only to a more intense competition for employment, with the result that wages will again be forced down to the same old subsistence level.[1]

Like most advocates of *laissez-faire* Madison did not maintain a perfect consistency in regard to all phases of that theory. For example, he believed that in a well-ordered republic the government should construct canals, turnpikes, and other internal improvements. In the Constitutional Convention he had recommended that Congress be vested with a general power to incorporate for those objects.[2] As President he called the attention of Congress on two occasions to the signal advantages to be derived from a general system of internal communication and conveyance.[3] One of his last official acts as chief executive was to veto a bill for internal improvements; not, however, for reasons of general policy, but on constitutional grounds. He reiterated his conviction of the desirability of such improvements, but he insisted that a constitutional amendment would be necessary to give Congress power to provide for them.[4] Nor did he alter his conviction on this subject after his retirement from the Presidency. In 1831, in a letter to Reynolds Chapman, he wrote, "Railroads, canals, and turnpikes are at once the criteria of a wise policy and the causes of national prosperity. The want of them will be a

[1] Letter to N. P. Trist, April, 1827, *Writings* (Cong. ed.), vol. III, p. 587.

[2] Farrand, *Records of the Federal Convention*, vol. II, p. 325.

[3] Richardson, *op. cit.*, vol. I, pp. 497, 567.

[4] *Ibid.*, vol. I, p. 585.

reproach to our republican system."[1] It may be pertinent to add that Madison's views on this matter were not in conflict with those of his famous predecessor in the Presidential office. Visions of a surplus in the national treasury had inspired Jefferson to ask: "Shall it lie unproductive in the public vaults? Shall the revenue be reduced? Or shall it rather be appropriated to the improvement of canals, rivers, education, and other great foundations of prosperity and union?"[2]

In the early period of his public career Madison had been opposed to protective tariffs as a means of stimulating domestic manufactures. He believed that an ample development of industry would come of itself as the needs of the country justified it. He did not accept the argument of the necessity of self-sufficiency in time of war, for he pointed out that in any future war there would be no lack of opportunity to procure fabricated goods from neutral countries.[3] Even to the end of his life he continued to affirm a theoretic devotion to universal freedom of trade, "which unites all nations, makes every man a citizen of the whole society of mankind, and perfects the good aimed at by the social union and constitutional government."[4] He believed commercial shackles to be generally unjust, inexpedient, and oppressive. He argued that if industry and commerce were allowed to take their own course, they would in the main be directed to those objects for which

[1] *Writings* (Hunt ed.), vol. IX, p. 437.

[2] Quoted by Charles E. Hill, "James Madison, Secretary of State," *The American Secretaries of State and Their Diplomacy*, Samuel F. Bemis, editor, vol. III, p. 143.

[3] Letter to Edmund Pendleton, Jan. 9, 1787, *Writings* (Hunt ed.), vol. II, pp. 306-7.

[4] Manuscript, *Madison Papers*, Library of Congress.

they are best suited and likely to be the most productive. The good of the whole society can be promoted best by allowing each individual to pursue his own interest and to perform those tasks for which he is best fitted.[1] The wealth of each and therefore the wealth of the whole will be best enhanced by freedom to order production as enlightened self-interest may dictate. Whenever manufacturing promises more profit than agriculture or commerce, its establishments will increase rapidly enough without the patronage of the state.[2] "It would be of no advantage," he observed, "to the shoemaker to make his own clothes to save the expense of the tailor's bill, nor of the tailor to make his own shoes to save the expense of procuring them from the shoemaker. It would be better policy to suffer each of them to employ his talents in his own way. Thus all are benefited by exchange, and the less this exchange is cramped by the government, the greater are the proportions of benefit to each. The same argument holds good between nation and nation, and between parts of the same nation."[3]

On the other hand Madison was accustomed at times to offer so many exceptions to these principles as to make himself almost a thoroughgoing protectionist. He appeared to feel the necessity of a well-rounded economic life as essential to national strength and safety, and he feared that without the stimulus of protective tariffs manufacturing would fail to keep pace with the growth of agriculture and commerce. He seemed to have visions of a national self-

[1] *Annals of Congress,* vol. I, pp. 111-12.

[2] Letter to Henry Clay, April, 1824, *Writings* (Hunt ed.), vol. IX, p. 124.

[3] *Annals of Congress,* vol. I, p. 112.

sufficiency in which the manufactures of the North would complement the agriculture of the South. Thus the whole republic would be independent of foreign supplies. The tariff would then cease to be a cause of discord, and a bond of economic interest would eventually unite the two sections of the country.[1] Moreover, he was disturbed by the prospect of a time when it would be difficult to find export markets for American agricultural products.[2] He attributed the depressed conditions of agriculture in his native State in the 1820's and '30's to the rapid development of farming in the Western country. He repeatedly adverted to the fact that foreign and domestic markets alike were glutted with the products of the soil, and that this condition would become worse unless surplus labor in this country could be diverted into manufacturing. He hoped for a nicely adjusted balance between the agricultural and industrial interests as one of the best ways of allaying sectional discontent.[3]

In Madison's view the policy of perfect freedom of international trade is based on two false premises. In the first place it is based on the assumption of a reciprocal attitude on the part of all other nations. However, nations with highly developed industry do not hesitate to impose every obstacle they can against the growth of manufacturing elsewhere.[4] In the second place the policy of free trade is

[1] Letter to Henry Clay, April 12, 1833, *Writings* (Cong. ed.), vol. IV, p. 567.

[2] Letter to Tench Coxe, March 20, 1820, *Writings* (Cong. ed.), vol. III, pp. 170-71.

[3] Letter to Professor Davis, 1832, *Writings* (Cong. ed.), vol. IV, pp. 264-65.

[4] Letter to Joseph C. Cabell, Sept. 18, 1828, *Writings* (Hunt ed.), vol. IX, pp. 317-18.

predicated on the illusion of perpetual peace, but the history of nations in modern times reveals that the years of peace have been equaled or exceeded in number by the years of war.[1]

Fortunately Madison wrote in very definite terms of the exceptions he would make to the "let alone" policy so far as concerned manufactures. He argued that industrial establishments which have already been created by State patronage in this country ought not to be allowed to perish. It would be "cruel" to neglect them and force their enterprise into other channels. Men cannot readily shift from one employment to another without suffering evil consequences from the readjustment.[2] In the second place articles necessary for national defense may well be regarded as suitable objects of protection. No nation ought to have to depend on another for articles essential to its safety. "The implements of industry used in procuring the necessaries of life" and commodities "too indispensable to be subjected to foreign contingencies" ought in like manner to be secured by national protection.[3] Finally, desirable manufactures which would never come into existence at all without government aid, but which once introduced would flourish without that aid, ought to be made the beneficiaries of state patronage in the form of protective tariffs.[4]

Madison's official acts as a member of Congress and as President betrayed a similar attitude in regard to govern-

[1] Letter to Matthew Carey, May 26, 1821, Manuscript, *Madison Papers*, Library of Congress.

[2] *Annals of Congress*, vol. I, p. 113.

[3] Manuscript, *Madison Papers*, Library of Congress.

[4] Letter to Henry Clay, April, 1824, *Writings* (Hunt ed.), vol. IX, p. 185.

ment intervention in economic matters. In the First Congress he proposed a small specific duty on all beer imported and expressed the hope that it would be sufficient "to induce the manufacture to take deep root in every State in the Union."[1] In 1794 he introduced a series of resolutions recommending tariffs on a number of products, notably leather goods, metal products, and textiles. The chief purpose was to be retaliation against countries discriminating against our commerce, but there was to be the additional purpose of increasing the "encouragement on such articles as we can produce within ourselves."[2] He also advocated tonnage duties on foreign vessels landing in our ports, so as to build up an American merchant marine large enough to provide transport facilities for all of our products, and to augment our naval strength in case of war.[3] He admitted, however, that the latter reason was the controlling one, and that if it were not for the question of national security involved, he would be in favor of throwing wide open the doors of our commerce to the shipping of all nations without discrimination of any kind.[4] So frequently he was torn between his predilections for *laissez-faire* and his interest in national strength and security.

In his first message to Congress, on May 23, 1809, Madison as chief executive advised the legislators that it would be "worthy of their just and provident care to make such further alteration in the laws as will more especially protect and foster the several branches of manu-

[1] *Annals of Congress*, vol. I, p. 145.
[2] *Ibid.*, vol. III, pp. 155-57.
[3] *Ibid.*, vol. I, p. 189.
[4] *Ibid.*, vol. I, p. 237.

facture which have been recently instituted or extended by the laudable exertions of our citizens."[1] He repeated this advice in a number of later communications.[2] His seventh annual message must have given considerable aid and comfort to even the most ardent protectionists. He observed that however wise the theory may be which would leave to the enlightened self-interest of individuals the ordering of the economic life of the country, divers exceptions have to be made. In the first place the theory implies a reciprocal adoption by other countries, which he pointed out was not the fact. In the second place experience has shown that so many conditions must conspire to introduce and develop manufacturing establishments, especially of the more complicated kinds, that a country may long remain without them if it is to depend solely upon the energy and resources of individuals. No longer did he stress entirely self-sufficiency in time of war. He pointed out that "with a protection not more than is due" to the enterprising owners, industry would become, at an early date, not only safe from competition from abroad, "but a source of domestic wealth and even of external commerce." He maintained that in selecting the industries best entitled to public patronage, preference should be given not only to such as would relieve the United States from dependence upon foreign supplies, but also to those providing for the primary wants of individuals, and to such as consumed the raw materials of American agriculture.[3]

It is only fair to add that Madison always introduced various qualifications into his advocacy of protectionist legis-

[1] Richardson, *op. cit.*, vol. I, pp. 469-70.

[2] *Ibid.*, vol. I, pp. 485, 495.

[3] *Ibid.*, vol. I, p. 567.

lation. He had no desire to see a pampered industrial capitalism brought into existence in this country. Apparently his dominant purpose was to preserve a reasonable balance between conflicting interests, so as to increase the economic vigor of the nation and eliminate sources of internal disaffection. And he could appeal for support in this to the example of Jefferson, who in the last year of his Presidency had recommended "the encouragement of manufactures to the extent of our own consumption at least, in all articles of which we raise the raw material," and had declared the prosperity of the country to rest upon a "due balance between agriculture, manufactures, and commerce."[1] Furthermore, Madison insisted that every tariff bill should be of limited duration,[2] and he maintained that in every doubtful case the government ought scrupulously to avoid any encouragement to a manufacturing interest, particularly where one part of the community would be favored at the expense of another.[3]

Madison's general theory of the state did not present a perfectly clear and logical view of political society and its organs. One is tempted to think that its author must on occasions have scorned consistency as "the hobgoblin of small minds." Generally he wrote in a rather cynical vein of human nature and distrusted man as a selfish animal, although at other times he was disposed to trust the wisdom

[1] Letter to Thomas Leiper, Jan. 21, 1809, *Writings of Jefferson* (Ford ed.), vol. IX, p. 239; see also Jefferson's first inaugural, Richardson, *op. cit.*, vol. I, p. 323.

[2] *Annals of Congress*, vol. I, p. 347.

[3] Letter to Thomas Cooper, March 23, 1824, *Writings* (Hunt ed.), vol. IX, p. 180.

and patriotism of ordinary mortals. He stressed the importance of liberty, but he avowed the protection of property to be the chief object of government, and he insisted upon a coercive state as a prerequisite to order and stability. He believed in the right of revolution, but he practically denied that right to the inhabitants of the individual States in the American Union in so far as it might involve a change from the republican form. He was theoretically devoted to economic individualism and enlightened self-interest, but the seductions of economic nationalism led him astray into advocacy of a very considerable protectionism.

Perhaps these contradictions will not be so difficult to understand if it is kept in mind that his ideas were the product of a time when political conditions were in a state of flux. Most of his theory was formed after the period of Revolution had come to a close. He had lived through that period, however, and had played an active, though minor, part in it. As a result his thinking was bound to have been colored by its basic doctrines. The conditions of the succeeding period, nevertheless, exerted the dominant influence. The attention of the more prosperous classes was now being centered upon the problem of creating a stronger national system and upon the dangers of anarchy and instability. In a similar way the years that followed, at the close of the eighteenth century and the beginning of the nineteenth, were destined to produce conflicting influences. The assumptions of the old *Naturrecht* philosophy were being questioned, and a vague tendency to think of the state as something more than a collection of atoms was becoming evident. The rise of an American nationalism, as expressed in the Louisiana Purchase and in the expansionism that led ultimately to the War of 1812, had its effect even upon Jefferson. That a political philosopher, as actively connected with events as Madison was, should have maintained perfect consistency in the face of such a rapidly shifting political scene is probably too much to expect.

THREE

# Views on Democracy

THE subject of this chapter involves first of all a matter of definition. In the modern age the term democracy in the political sense has generally been defined in either of two ways. Since about 1825 it has usually been understood to mean the sovereignty of the majority, with few if any restrictions upon the right of the majority to put its will into effect. Thus defined, it has generally implied universal manhood suffrage, direct election of all of the principal officers of government, frequent elections, some degree of direct government, at least to the extent of popular referenda on constitutional changes, and, finally, an abiding faith in the political wisdom and virtue of the masses. In this form, as an American ideal, it has had as its principal source the Jacksonian Revolution of the 1820's.

There has also been an older and broader definition, perhaps comprising all of the meaning given to the term by Harold J. Laski when he defined it as "The effort of men to affirm their own essence and to remove all barriers to that affirmation."[1] At any rate democracy in this broader sense has certainly included such ideals as the abolition of privilege, the condemnation of slavery, equality before the law, freedom of speech, press, religion, and assemblage, a regard for "the eminent dignity of man," and abundant

[1] "Democracy," *Encyclopedia of the Social Sciences*, vol. V, p. 76.

protection for the rights of minorities, as well as opportunity for expression of the majority will. Democracy according to this definition has not assumed the validity of the maxim, *Vox populi, vox Dei.* On the contrary it has been predicated upon notions of a "higher law" of reason and universal right, existing as a limitation upon all government. Its proponents have been as suspicious of the absolute sovereignty of the majority as of the exercise of any other kind of unlimited power. In a word, it has been virtually synonymous with liberalism.

### ATTITUDE TOWARD THE SOVEREIGNTY OF THE MASSES

As a democrat according to the first of these definitions, Madison could scarcely be given a very good rating, although perhaps not such an inferior one as is commonly assigned to him. To begin with, he did not believe in the unrestricted sovereignty of the majority. As early as 1786 he wrote that the multiplicity, mutability, and injustice of the laws of republics bring into question the whole theory that the majority who rule in such governments are the safest guardians of public good and private rights. How is a majority, he asked, united by an apparent interest and a common passion, to be restrained from unjust infringements of the rights of minorities and individuals? By respect for character? However strong this motive may be in individuals, its efficacy is reduced in proportion to the number who are to share the praise or blame. Besides, it is in itself dependent upon public opinion; and in popularly governed societies public opinion is merely the opinion of the majority, that is, of the very group whose conduct is to be measured by it. Will religion restrain the majority intent upon an illegitimate interest? It is not even an effective restraint upon individuals, much less upon groups of individuals.[1] Writing to James Monroe in the same year, Madison declared "There is no maxim which is more liable to be misapplied . . . than the current one that the interest of the majority is the political standard of right and wrong." In effect it can only mean the assumption of the vicious principle that force is the measure of right.[2] In the Virginia ratifying convention of 1788 he maintained that the destruction of republics, both ancient and modern, has generally resulted from the hatred and discord growing out of majority tyranny over the rights of minorities.[3]

Those who advocate a simple democracy, according to Madison, or a pure republic governed by majority rule assume an altogether fictitious situation. They assume that the people composing the society enjoy not only an equality of political rights, but that they have a precise identity of interests and the same feelings in every respect. The majority interest would be the interest of the minority also. Questions of policy would be decided according to the majority judgment concerning the good of the whole. But in reality no community is so homogeneous. Civilized societies inevitably become divided into various groups and classes based upon conflicting economic interests. In addition to these natural divisions, artificial ones also develop founded upon differences in political, religious, and miscellaneous opinions. Combinations and alliances are formed among these groups on divers sorts of bargains, so that what passes

[1] Vices of the Political System of the United States, *Writings* (Hunt ed.), vol. II, pp. 366-68.

[2] *Ibid.*, vol. II, p. 273.

[3] Elliot, *Debates*, vol. II, p. 90.

for an expression of the will of the majority regarding the general good represents in reality a concerted scheming for factious advantage.[1]

Instead of defending the absolute sovereignty of the majority, Madison detested it so strongly that he sought in almost every conceivable way to prevent its exercise. As a disciple of Locke he set up the presumption, first of all, of liberty and property as natural rights which the state, no matter what its organization, cannot invade.[2] One of his principal reasons for advocating a national government in the United States of considerable strength was to frustrate the ambitions of reckless majorities in the State legislatures,[3] and his scheme of checks and balances in the Federal government was designed largely to prevent domination by the legislative branch,[4] the agency most likely to reflect the popular will. His theory of representation did not contemplate that device as a means of giving more efficient expression to the desires of the majority, but rather as a means of "refining and enlarging the public views" by passing them through the minds of a select few, whose intelligence and virtue would discern the good of the whole better than the people themselves could do.[5] His suggestions for controlling the spirit of faction were also designed to check too immediate an expression of popular ambitions. He believed it essential to play one faction off

[1] Letter to Jefferson, Oct. 24, 1787, *Writings* (Hunt ed.), vol. V, pp. 28-29.

[2] John Locke, *Second Essay on Civil Government* (Everyman ed.), p. 185.

[3] *Federalist* (Lodge ed.), No. 44, pp. 278-79.

[4] *Ibid.*, No. 48, p. 309.

[5] *Ibid.*, No. 10, p. 57.

against another in Machiavellian fashion,[1] and to extend the territorial sphere of government so that the people would be broken up into so many conflicting interests and parties that a common sentiment could hardly ever be felt by a majority.[2]

But even these numerous recommendations did not exhaust the list of Madison's remedies against the rule of the majority. In the Philadelphia Convention he urged the adoption of fairly long terms of office for members of the national legislature—three years for Representatives and nine years for Senators—so that they might have sufficient independence and firmness to "intervene against impetuous counsels."[3] He denied that tenure of such length would be dangerous to liberty; on the contrary it would be one of its best safeguards. By correcting the infirmities of popular government, a relatively permanent legislation would prevent disgust with popular rule that might culminate in a movement toward despotism.[4] The Presidential veto he thought could well be employed also as a means of preventing "popular or factious injustice," and he urged that the Convention should adopt a requirement of a three-fourths vote in both houses of Congress to override executive disapproval of a proposed law.[5]

Most of all, Madison would have relied upon the existence of an upper house to protect the people against

[1] "Parties," *National Gazette;* reprinted in *Writings* (Hunt ed.), vol. VI, p. 86.

[2] Letter to Jefferson, Oct. 24, 1787, *Writings* (Hunt ed.), vol. V, p. 31.

[3] Farrand, *Records of the Federal Convention,* vol. II, pp. 214, 421.

[4] *Writings* (Hunt ed.), vol. V, pp. 284-85.

[5] Farrand, *Records of the Federal Convention,* vol. II, p. 587.

themselves. In Number 52 of the *Federalist*, which he claimed to have written, reference was made to the tendency of all single assemblies to yield to sudden and violent impulses "and to be seduced by factious leaders into intemperate and pernicious resolutions."[1] Moreover, the time will come, the author maintained, when greater extremes of wealth and poverty will characterize the American nation. With an increasing population there will be a larger proportion who will labor as hewers of wood and drawers of water and secretly long for a more equitable distribution of life's blessings. Under a republic with substantially equal privileges of suffrage, power will gravitate into the hands of this least prosperous element. "Symptoms of a levelling spirit," he asserted, "have sufficiently appeared already to give notice of the impending danger." How can this danger be guarded against? "Among other means by the establishment of a body in the government sufficiently respectable for its wisdom and virtue, to aid on such emergencies, the preponderance of justice by throwing its weight into that scale."[2] Alexander Hamilton or John Adams could scarcely have made a more candid avowal of aristocratic inclinations.

It should be added, however, that while Madison condemned the sovereignty of the majority, he was just as emphatically opposed to government by a minority, at least in its more obvious forms. Despotism of any sort was repugnant to him, whether of the few or of the many; and sometimes in his zeal for combating the former, he almost went to the extreme of advocating the latter. He was addicted on occasions to referring in glowing terms to the

[1] Lodge edition, p. 388.

[2] Farrand, *Records of the Federal Convention*, vol. I, pp. 421-23.

ideal of popular rule, although he certainly did not mean all that would now be conveyed by that phrase. In Number 39 of the *Federalist* he commended a republic as the only form of government that could ever be reconciled with the genius of the people of America, with the fundamental principles of the Revolution, and with that resolve in the mind of every apostle of liberty that all our political experiments shall rest on the capacity of mankind for self-government.[1] As a member of Congress he proposed the following declaration as the first amendment to the Constitution: "That all power is originally vested in, and consequently derived from, the people, that government is instituted and ought to be exercised for the benefit of the people, which consists in the enjoyment of life and liberty, with the right of acquiring and using property, and generally of pursuing and obtaining happiness and safety; that the people have an indubitable, inalienable, and indefeasible right to reform their government, whenever it be found adverse or inadequate to the purposes of its institution."[2]

During the Philadelphia Convention and later, Madison proposed a number of safeguards against minority domination. He urged the adoption of measures to prevent election of a President by the representatives of less than a majority of the people in case the election should be thrown into the lower house of Congress.[3] He opposed a proposal to have the Constitution adopted by the concurrence of nine States, lest that might mean its being put into force

[1] Lodge edition, p. 246.

[2] *Annals of Congress*, vol. I, pp. 433-34.

[3] Farrand, *Records of the Federal Convention*, vol. II, pp. 527, 536.

over the whole body of the people, though less than a majority of them should have ratified it.[1] He insisted upon proportionate representation of the States in the Senate, for otherwise a minority of the people would be able to negative the will of a majority.[2] In 1823 he advised changing the method of electing the President in the event of failure of any candidate to receive a majority of the electoral votes. He advocated submitting the election to a joint session of the Senate and the House, with each member voting as an individual. He opposed the existing method of election by the House of Representatives, voting by States, as too great "a departure from the republican principle of numerical equality."[3]

In addition he believed direct popular election of some agencies of the government essential as a check upon minority tyranny and as a means of preserving the republican character of the system. He admitted in the Convention his advocacy of a "policy of refining the popular appointments by successive filtrations," but he feared that this might be carried too far. He would confine it to the selection of the second branch of the legislature and perhaps the executive and the judiciary. He believed that "the great fabric to be raised would be more stable and durable, if it should rest on the solid foundation of the people themselves . . ."[4] In a later speech in the Convention he even declared himself in favor of popular election of the national executive in principle. Such a method, he thought, would be

NB

[1] *Ibid.*, vol. II, p. 469.

[2] *Ibid.*, vol. II, pp. 8-10.

[3] Letter to George Hay, Aug. 23, 1823, *Writings* (Hunt ed.), vol. IX, p. 151.

[4] Farrand, *Records of the Federal Convention*, vol. I, pp. 49-50.

as likely as any that could be devised to produce a magistrate of distinguished character. The suffrages of the people generally could only be attracted by a candidate of sufficient merit to become widely known and an object of general esteem.[1] Although he later decided in favor of selection of the President by an electoral college, mainly, as he averred, because of the practical problem of a wider diffusion of the franchise in the Northern States than in the South, he continued to maintain his theoretical preference for popular election.[2]

But Madison did not look with an excess of favor upon direct participation by the people in government. He referred in *Federalist* Number 10 to a pure democracy, which he defined as one in which the citizens enact and administer the laws directly, as one of the worst forms of government.[3] In the Federal Convention of 1787 he insisted upon ratification of the new Constitution by conventions in the States elected by the people. He urged this method not because it would be more democratic, but because he regarded the people in the States, not the State governments, as the real sovereigns;[4] and of course also for the reason that he did not trust the legislatures to pass judgment on a Constitution that would deprive them of important powers. Furthermore, he said nothing about the desirability of submitting the question of ratification or rejection to a popular referendum, which would have been the truly democratic procedure.

In 1790 Madison wrote a long reply to Jefferson's

[1] *Ibid.*, vol. II, pp. 56-57.
[2] *Ibid.*, vol. II, pp. 56-57; 110-11.
[3] Lodge edition, p. 56.
[4] Farrand, *Records of the Federal Convention*, vol. II, p. 476.

famous letter advocating periodic submission of constitutions and laws to the people for approval, revision, or repeal. Jefferson believed that no one generation had any right to bind succeeding generations, and that therefore no constitution or law should continue in force for more than about twenty years unless reapproved at the end of that period by the people.[1] Madison thought the idea a good one from the standpoint of pure theory, but he maintained that there were serious practical objections that could be adduced against it. If applied to a constitution, the government would automatically come to an end at a given time, unless prolonged by a previous constitutional act. But the nation would always be confronted by the danger of an interregnum with all the confusion incident thereto. In the case of ordinary laws a similar difficulty would obtain. Unless they were kept in force by other laws anticipating their expiration, all rights depending upon positive laws, especially the rights of property, would become defunct, and violent struggles would occur between the parties interested in reviving, and those interested in overthrowing, the previous distribution of property. Moreover, frequent submission of constitutions and laws to revision would agitate the public mind more frequently and more violently than necessary, and popular esteem for a government too mutable and novel would be diminished.[2]

In order to avoid such embarrassments, Madison thought it would be better to rely upon the doctrine of tacit assent to justify the right of one generation to bind generations to come. That is, succeeding generations would, of course, have the right to revoke the political acts of their forebears;

[1] *Writings of Jefferson* (Ford ed.), vol. V, p. 115.

[2] *Writings* (Hunt ed.), vol. V, pp. 436-40 note.

but unless they exercised this right it should be assumed that they gave tacit approval to those acts.[1] He neglected to consider the vast difference between a positive act of repealing a law and deciding whether a law which had automatically expired should be revived. The weight of inertia and the force of the habit of obedience, the extreme conservatism of the bulk of mankind, would have much more influence in the former case than in the latter. The contrasting attitudes of the two philosophers on this question illustrated about as neatly as anything could their divergent temperaments. Jefferson, the idealist, cherished what was theoretically desirable, and minimized or ignored the practical difficulties. In his judgment a bit of confusion and uncertainty was not a high price to pay for liberty. Madison, the realist, respected the theory, but magnified the practical difficulties. For him stability and the rights of property came pretty close to being the all-important considerations.

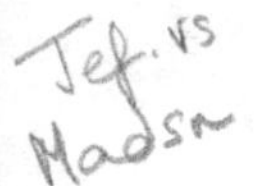


[1] *Ibid.*, vol. V, p. 440 note. On the other hand, in a letter to Caleb Wallace, Madison affirmed that a State constitution should provide for a convenient and relatively easy mode of revision. He suggested that a majority of any two of the three departments should have authority to call a plenipotentiary convention whenever they considered that their constitutional rights had been violated by the other department, or whenever they considered that an essential part of the constitution needed amendment. He declared such an arrangement as this to be particularly valuable in a new State, where it would be "imprudent and indecent" for a handful of early settlers to impose a frame of government, based on its limited experience and needs, upon what would later be a populous area with a higher state of development. He lamented the difficulty of amending the constitution of Virginia and observed that unless a constitution contained some principle making revision necessary and certain, it would probably never be changed. *Ibid.*, vol. II, pp. 175-76.

Madison's views on the suffrage also reflected the basic conflict in his mind between democratic and aristocratic inclinations. He often referred to his theoretic prepossessions in favor of a universal franchise. In the Philadelphia Convention he declared the right to vote to be "one of the fundamental articles of republican government."[1] In his *Autobiography*, written about the year 1830, he affirmed his belief that the suffrage ought to be extended so far "as to secure in every event and change in the state of society a majority of people on the side of power. A government resting on a minority is an aristocracy, not a republic, and could not be safe with a numerical and physical force against it without a standing army, an enslaved press, and a disarmed populace."[2]

On the other hand, the right to property, especially property in land, was a veritable obsession with Madison. For him the possession of a freehold estate was at once the emblem of stability, the badge of respectability, and the evidence of political capacity. The right to such possession sprang from the law of nature and was therefore coeval with eternal justice. Since it was the primary duty of government to protect this right, no apportionment of the franchise could ever justly be made that would endanger it. But wholly aside from the question of justice, the security of liberty itself, according to Madison, depends upon protection for the rights of property in the distribution of the suffrage. If all power be allowed to the indigent masses, one of two things will certainly happen: either they will yield to blind passion in legislative attacks upon the more prosperous minority, or else they will become the dupes

[1] Farrand, *Records of the Federal Convention*, vol. II, p. 203.
[2] Manuscript, *Madison Papers*, Library of Congress.

of wealthy miscreants ambitious for power. In either case liberty will be overthrown: in the first by a despotism, the natural fruit of anarchy; in the second, by an oligarchy based upon corruption.[1]

The best expression of Madison's views on the suffrage is undoubtedly to be found in his famous speech of August 7 in the Federal Convention and in the note which he appended to that speech about 1821. He avowed the right of suffrage to be an essential provision in a republican constitution. But he maintained that extreme care must be exercised as to the apportionment of that right. Allow it exclusively to property, and the rights of persons may be oppressed. Extend it equally to all, and the rights of property may be trampled upon by indigent majorities.[2] Like Gouverneur Morris he feared that the time was not far distant when the great majority of Americans would have neither landed nor any other form of property, or worse still, they would become the dupes and retainers of their capitalist employers and vote not as free men, but in obedience to the dictates of powerful magnates to whom they owed their livelihood.[3] In the latter case the interests of true wealth, especially of landed property, would be at the mercy of the speculators and money changers.

He was disposed to advocate, therefore, some plan by which landholders could enjoy an added degree of representation besides their representation as persons. He thought this could be done by confining the suffrage for one branch of the legislature to freeholders, and admitting all others

[1] *Writings* (Cong. ed.), vol. I, p. 188.

[2] Farrand, *Records of the Federal Convention*, vol. II, pp. 203-4; 204 note.

[3] *Ibid.*, vol. III, pp. 451-52, Appendix A, CCCXLII.

to a common right with freeholders in electing the other branch; or by an enlargement of the election district and an extended term of service for one branch. He believed that large districts would be favorable to the choice of men of "general respectability" and "of probable attachment to the rights of property." But if neither of these devices should be found practicable, and if the alternative should lie between universal suffrage for both branches and restriction of the entire right to a part of the citizens, then he would favor universal suffrage; for it would be better that those having interests of property and persons both at stake should be deprived of half of their share, than that those having personal rights only should be deprived of the whole.[1] It was his hope that some kind of a balance could be achieved in which the interests of both could be represented. In this way the republican ideal of a wide extension of the franchise would be harmonized with the practical necessity of protecting the rights of property.

In spite of his agrarian sympathies Madison did not desire to convert the government of the United States into a landholding oligarchy. When a proposal was made in the Constitutional Convention to require possession of landed property as a qualification for membership in the national legislature, he opposed it. Landed possessions, he maintained, are no certain evidence of wealth, for they may be encumbered by debts greater than their actual worth. The unjust laws of the States were instigated by this class of debtors more than by any other. In addition it is "politic as well as just that the interests and rights of every class should be duly represented and understood in the public

[1] *Ibid.*, vol. III, pp. 454-55, Appendix A, CCCXLII.

councils." He pointed out that the three principal classes which the population of this country comprises are the landed, the commercial, and the manufacturing. Although the last two are not so numerous as the first, in time they will become so; and it would be unjust to include in the organic law a provision depriving them of representation.[1]

Although he asserted in the *Federalist* that all political experiments should rest on the capacity of mankind for self-government,[2] Madison did not have a very exalted opinion of the political wisdom and virtue of the masses. In a letter to Edmund Randolph in 1788 he wrote, "There can be no doubt that there are subjects to which the capacities of the bulk of mankind are unequal, and on which they must and will be governed by those with whom they happen to have acquaintance and confidence."[3] More than this, the masses are the chronic victims of factious tendencies, of violent hatreds and transient impulses that often lead them to desire defective and unnecessary laws which are altogether too difficult to repeal even after time and reflection have shown them to be unwise. These evils increase the expense of government, multiply litigation between individuals, and impair that certainty and stability which are among the chief essentials of a well-ordered state.[4] As much as anything else it was this conviction, that the masses are generally impetuous and prone to envy and contention, that was at the bottom of Madison's distrust of democracy in the sense of majority rule.

[1] *Ibid.*, vol. II, pp. 123-24.

[2] Lodge edition, No. 39, p. 246.

[3] *Writings* (Hunt ed.), vol. V, pp. 81-82.

[4] Letter to John Cartwright, 1824, *Writings* (Hunt ed.), vol. IX, pp. 181-82.

VIEW OF DEMOCRACY IN THE BROADER SENSE

As indicated at the beginning of this chapter, democracy has had another and broader meaning. It has been the expression of a tradition that stemmed originally from Cicero and the Stoics and was carried forward by medievalists like Isidore of Seville, John of Salisbury, Marsiglio of Padua, and John Gerson, and in more modern times by such famous opponents of absolutism as Francis Hotman, John Milton, James Harrington, and John Locke. Under the aegis of this tradition democracy has emphasized individual rights and the protection of minorities fully as much if not more than it has the sovereignty of the people and the common welfare. The major concern of its exponents has been to defend the common man against oppression resulting from the exercise of political power founded upon privilege and inequality—in other words, to combat monarchy and hereditary aristocracy, and to insist that government should rest upon the informed consent of the governed. Perhaps it is on this basis alone that the philosophers of what is essentially a liberal ideal can justly be called democrats.

That Madison was very definitely a representative of democracy in this broader sense must be apparent already from what has been said respecting his views of sovereignty and the bases of political power. Absolutism, whatever its form, was the *bête noire* of his mind, and natural rights, especially the right of property, were the sacred heritage of civilized man and the principal subjects of the law of nature. Some additional observations are necessary to present a complete picture of his democratic theory in this larger sense. His views on slavery, natural rights, freedom of expression, and opposition to war and militarism will need to be considered since they may be taken to exemplify a general attitude of regard for liberty, equality, and protection of the common man against arbitrary government.

From the time of the Stoics philosophers of the democratic tradition had recognized a fundamental inconsistency between the law of nature, as the embodiment of eternal right and justice, and the institution of slavery. That one man should own another could scarcely be reconciled with the idea of the natural equality of all men. Although the Stoics and some of their successors tolerated the existence of the institution, they never sought to justify it on theoretical grounds, and most of them would have welcomed its speedy extinction. This was essentially the attitude of the democratic philosophers in America in the late eighteenth and early nineteenth centuries.

Madison was born into a slaveholding environment, and he continued to own slaves until the end of his life. He treated them, however, with a consideration bordering upon indulgence.[1] He never sold any of them until two years before his death, when straitened circumstances compelled him to dispose of several, with their own consent, to certain of his kinsmen.[2] Furthermore, on several occasions he expressed his philosophic convictions against the institution. In the Philadelphia Convention he opposed a twenty-year limitation on the power of Congress to forbid the importation of slaves on the ground that such a long term would be "dishonorable to the national charac-

[1] Hunt, *Life of Madison*, pp. 380-81.

[2] Letter to Edward Coles, 1834, manuscript, *Madison Papers*, Library of Congress.

ter."[1] But in addition he thought it wrong to "admit in the Constitution the idea that there could be property in human beings."[2] In a letter to Lafayette in 1826 he deplored the fact that the presence of slavery in the American republic impaired the influence of our political example.[3] In the Virginia constitutional convention of 1829 he declared it to be essential to justice, to humanity, to the sympathies of human nature, to the integrity of the national character that those who belonged to the class of slaves should be considered as much as possible in the light of human beings and not as mere property.[4]

But while he regarded slavery as an evil which ought to be abolished, it was foreign to his temperament to lead a crusade against it or to demand its immediate extirpation by drastic methods. He believed that peaceful and gradual methods were the best means of getting rid of any deeply rooted evil. In 1819 in a letter to Robert J. Evans he recommended a solution for the slave problem which he considered at once humane and just. He proposed that a sufficient acreage of the lands belonging to the United States should be sold over a period of years to provide for the gradual purchase of slaves from their masters. The negroes thus redeemed from bondage would be transported to a colony to be established in Africa. Certain exceptions would have to be made. Blacks who preferred to remain in slavery rather than face the uncertainties of life in a strange environment would be permitted to do so. Slaves who had been disabled or worn out

[1] Farrand, *Records of the Federal Convention*, vol. II, p. 415.
[2] *Ibid.*, vol. II, p. 417.
[3] *Writings* (Hunt ed.), vol. IX, p. 266.
[4] *Ibid.*, vol. IX, p. 362.

in the service of their masters would remain a charge upon their former owners. And then Madison offered one other exception which probably would have been fatal to the whole scheme: servants whom their masters regarded as too valuable to be disposed of at the price fixed by due process of law would not need to be sold.[1]

Madison opposed the Missouri Compromise and other attempts to prevent the spread of slavery. He believed that an uncontrolled dispersion of the total number of slaves would be best, not only for the nation, but for the slaves themselves. The fewer the number of slaves in proportion to the rest of the population in a given area, the better their prospects for an improved condition and for emancipation.[2] But to the end of his life the method that appealed to him as the most practicable for eliminating the evil was emancipation through purchase by the national government, followed by colonization. In his will he bequeathed two thousand dollars to an organization dedicated to the promotion of that method, the American Colonization Society.[3]

During the contest over ratification of the Constitution Madison opposed the movement for adding a bill of rights to that instrument. This fact is sometimes taken to mean that he had no sympathy with the libertarian ideals of the Revolution, that he was concerned only with the protection of the property right, and cared little for such personal rights as freedom of the press and religion, trial by jury, and exemption from double jeopardy in criminal cases. Such a view can scarcely be maintained in

[1] *Writings* (Hunt ed.), vol. VIII, pp. 439-47.
[2] Letter to James Monroe, *Writings* (Hunt ed.), vol. IX, p. 25.
[3] *Writings* (Hunt ed.), vol. IX, p. 550.

the face of the facts. Madison's opposition to the movement for adding a bill of rights did not spring from an indifference to liberty, but from a desire to avoid confusion and delay in ratification, and from a concern for preventing every possible opportunity for an abuse of power. In the Virginia convention, for example, he argued that the inclusion of a bill of rights might be dangerous, to the extent that if an imperfect enumeration should be made, the implication might follow that everything omitted had been given to the general government.[1]

In a letter to Jefferson in October, 1788, Madison gave a more complete exposition of his views on the subject. He declared that there was always the danger that a positive declaration of the most essential rights might not be given sufficient latitude. He was convinced that the rights of conscience in particular, if submitted to majority definition, would be restricted in most undesirable fashion. A common objection of the masses in New England, he pointed out, was that the Constitution, by prohibiting religious tests for public office, opened the door for Jews, Turks, and infidels. Moreover, experience demonstrates, he claimed, the ineffectiveness of a bill of rights on the very occasions when its control is most needed. In Virginia the declaration of rights has been violated in every instance where it has been opposed by a willful majority. Wherever the real power of a government lies, there is the danger of oppression. "Wherever there is an interest and power to do wrong, wrong will generally be done, and not less readily by a powerful and interested party than by a powerful and interested prince."[2] What Madi-

[1] Elliot, *Debates*, vol. II, pp. 451-52.

[2] *Writings* (Hunt ed.), vol. V, p. 272.

son undoubtedly meant was that the real security to liberty lies in checks and balances which reduce the powers of government to the lowest minimum consistent with order and stability.

Still he thought a bill of rights has a certain value. The political principles declared in so solemn a manner eventually acquire the character of fundamental maxims of free government, and as they gain a wide and familiar acceptance, counteract the impulses of passion and interest. Moreover, although it is generally true that the danger of tyranny springs from determined majorities, yet there may be occasions when the evil proceeds from usurped powers of the government. A declaration of rights may be a convenient precaution against such possibilities, however remote they may appear to be. It is often alleged, he observed, that there is a tendency in all governments to augment their powers at the expense of liberty. But the premise is only partly true. Power when it has reached a certain degree of energy and independence does tend to augment itself by any convenient means. But below that degree the tendency is the reverse, that is, toward gradual relaxation, until the abuses of liberty compel a sudden swing in the opposite direction. Liberty, in other words, is equally endangered when governments have too much power and when they have too little. A proper mean between these extremes is the appropriate remedy to be sought.[1]

With the establishment of the new political system in 1789 Madison's fear of anarchy was supplanted by the other principal emotion that prompted most of his theory, namely, the fear of abuse of power. Consequently in the

[1] *Ibid.*, vol. V, pp. 271-74.

First Congress he became the leader of the very movement he had formerly opposed, the movement in favor of a bill of rights. He now declared that he wanted to render the Constitution "as acceptable to the whole people of the United States as it had been to a majority" [sic], to create the impression that the defenders of the new instrument were sincere votaries of liberty, and to guard against any possible abuses of power by the general government. He was not satisfied to stop there, however. He believed that there was danger of oppression from majorities in the particular States, even greater than had to be feared from any branch of the general government. Accordingly he proposed to include, along with the limitations upon the national government, prohibitions upon the States against violating freedom of conscience and the press and against deprivation of jury trial in criminal cases.[1]

As the years passed and the true significance of Federalist policies became apparent, Madison evinced more and more solicitude for protection of liberty against excess of power. Some of the assertions he made in Congress during this period would have done credit to Jefferson himself. He avowed, for example, that when a people form a constitution they reserve all those rights which they have not expressly delegated; and it is questionable whether Congress can even legislate respecting those rights, much less violate them.[2] He made it his special business to combat all attacks upon freedom of expression, even going so far as to defend the vituperative outbursts of the press and political clubs against the government dur-

[1] *Annals of Congress*, vol. I, pp. 431-32.
[2] *Ibid.*, vol. I, pp. 439-40.

ing the Whiskey Rebellion.[1] As a member of the Virginia House of Delegates in 1799 he maintained the same uncompromising attitude, denouncing the infamous Sedition Act for its denial of freedom of the press. He declared that "to the press alone, chequered as it is with abuses, the world is indebted for all the triumphs which have been gained by reason and humanity over error and oppression." He regarded the prohibition upon Congress in the First Amendment as absolute. To the question whether the Federal government does not even have the power to protect itself against libelous attacks, he replied with a categorical negative.[2] He denied the possibility of drawing a distinction between freedom and "licentiousness" of the press. No means have ever yet been devised, he insisted, by which the press can be corrected without being enslaved. A supposed freedom which admits of exceptions, alleged to be licentious, is not freedom at all.[3]

Needless to say, Madison condemned the Alien Act just as emphatically as he did its companion in infamy. But of course on different grounds. He maintained that it deprived persons of their rights to a judicial trial and the writ of habeas corpus. He denied the justice of empowering the President to revoke the admission of aliens without a judicial conviction of crime. Their admission to this country was a public grant of personal right, and there was no more propriety in an arbitrary revocation of such a grant than there would be in a similar revocation of a

[1] *Ibid.*, vol. IV, pp. 934-35.

[2] Report on the Virginia Resolutions, *Writings* (Hunt ed.), vol. VI, pp. 389-92.

[3] Address of the General Assembly to the People of the Commonwealth of Virginia, *Writings* (Hunt ed.), vol. VI, pp. 334-36.

grant of land.[1] Here we seem to have a rather interesting refutation of the thesis that Madison always exalted the rights of property above the rights of persons.

There was another species of liberty that engaged Madison's earnest attention, and that was liberty of religion. Absolute exemption of religion from any degree of political control was almost an obsession with him. He condemned the doctrine that without some alliance or coalition between church and state, neither can endure.[2] He maintained that complete separation of the two does more to foster true religion than all the religious establishments that have ever been devised.[3] Some of his other views were even more extreme. He disapproved of the appointment of chaplains to be paid out of the national treasury, suggesting that if any member of the legislature felt that he needed the spiritual ministrations of one of these, he should provide for them at his own expense. Finally, he objected to executive proclamations of religious fasts and festivals, unless in the form of mere recommendations to the people.[4]

Opposition to militarism and war has had a place of no small importance in the democratic ideal, broadly defined. The doctrine of Stoicism was essentially pacifist, and philosophers inheriting the Stoic tradition have ever since viewed with distrust the dominance of the military.

[1] Report on Virginia Resolutions, *Writings* (Hunt ed.), vol. VI, p. 363.

[2] Letter to Edward Livingston, 1822, *Writings* (Hunt ed.), vol. IX, p. 99.

[3] Letter to Edward Everett, 1823, *Writings* (Hunt ed.), vol. IX, p. 127.

[4] Letter to Edward Livingston, 1822, *Writings* (Hunt ed.), vol. IX, p. 99.

It was the privilege of Madison and Jefferson to represent this position in America. Both condemned a standing army as a menace to liberty and insisted upon a strict subordination of the military to the civil authority.[1] Madison condemned war as the most dreaded of all enemies to public liberty, "because it comprises and develops the germ of every other." It is the progenitor of armies and debts and taxes, and these are the favored instruments for establishing the domination of the few over the many. War is the corroding principle of republicanism producing, as it does, inequalities of fortune, opportunities for fraud, and executive tyranny.[2] But the same mind that conceived these excellent doctrines was able to affirm seventeen years later that the War of 1812 was "stamped with that justice which invites the smiles of Heaven on the means of conducting it to a successful termination."[3] Sweet are the uses not only of adversity, but also of political expediency.

Madison was not over-sanguine as to the possibility of ridding the world of the curse of war. Still he believed there was some hope, and that men ought to strive to their utmost to make that hope a reality. He suggested several remedies which he thought might be effective. For that class of wars which emanate from the mere will of absolutist governments the obvious cure would lie in enforcing responsibility of the government to the people. This would not be a panacea, for there would remain those

[1] Elliot, *Debates*, vol. II, p. 285; *Federalist* (Lodge ed.), No. 41, p. 251; Charles E. Merriam, *A History of American Political Theories*, New York, 1920, p. 172.

[2] Political Observations, manuscript, Columbia University Library.

[3] Richardson, *op. cit.*, vol. I, p. 524.

types of wars which germinate in the passions and prejudices of the people themselves. An efficacious mode of preventing these would be to compel each generation to bear the burden of its own wars, instead of allowing them to carry them on at the expense of future generations. In addition the taxes imposed to defray the cost of this type of war ought to bear as directly as possible upon the people themselves, so that those who pay them would really feel something of the penalty of rushing heedlessly into conflict and would not be deluded into permitting misapplications of their money. If such restraints were imposed, parsimony would be sure to checkmate ambition, and in the *impasse* that would result, reason might have a better chance to decide the issue for the public good.[1] He overlooked the fact that a government intent upon war might poison the minds of its citizens and seduce them into paying direct taxes as readily as they would purchase bonds. In fact he himself as President did not scruple to generate a little popular prejudice and passion in favor of a war with Great Britain.[2]

### MADISON'S THEORY AND "JEFFERSONIAN DEMOCRACY"

The concluding section of this chapter may well be devoted to a study of the question, Was Madison a true exponent of Jeffersonian democracy? There is a disposition on the part of many writers to imply that this question should be answered in the negative, to suggest that Jefferson's theory was so permeated with popular sympathy that Madi-

[1] "Universal Peace," *National Gazette*, Feb. 2, 1792; reprinted in *Writings* (Hunt ed.), vol. VI, pp. 88-90.

[2] *Supra*, pp. 22-23.

son could never have accepted it. Thus Professor Jacobson considers "confidence in majority rule" to be one of "the vital contributions to American political thought" made by the Sage of Monticello.[1] William E. Dodd declares that "Jefferson had a boundless faith in the masses."[2] And in the opinion of Professor Parrington, it was Jefferson's belief that "The cure for the evils of democracy was more democracy."[3]

But generalizations like these would seem to betray a rather uncritical view of Jefferson's philosophy. The idea that he was animated by "confidence in majority rule," for example, cannot be squared with several of his own assertions on the subject. In his Notes on Virginia he declared that "An elective despotism was not the government we fought for, but one which should not only be founded on free principles, but in which the powers of government should be so divided and balanced among bodies of magistracy, as that no one could transcend their legal limits, without being effectually checked and restrained by the others."[4] In other words, he believed in the good old system of checks and balances, which had always had as one of its main purposes the frustration of majority rule. In his first inaugural he admonished the nation to "bear in mind this sacred principle that though the will of the majority is in all cases to prevail, that will, to be rightful must be reasonable; that the minority possess their equal rights, which equal laws must protect, and to violate which

[1] J. Mark Jacobson, *The Development of American Political Thought*, New York, 1932, p. 247.

[2] *Statesmen of the Old South*, New York, 1911, p. 55.

[3] *Main Currents in American Thought*, vol. I, p. 354.

[4] *Writings of Jefferson* (Ford ed.), vol. II, p. 224.

would be oppression."[1] Moreover, he believed that he as President had a perfect right to pronounce the Sedition Act unconstitutional, and to nullify it, although it had been passed by an undoubted majority of the representatives of the people.[2] The conclusion seems inescapable that his conception of "majority rule" was essentially the same as that of Locke, that is, the will of the majority should prevail except in those cases where the natural rights of the individual are violated,[3] which is a pretty large qualification. Certainly he adhered to no dogma that the voice of the people is the voice of God.[4]

The statement that "Jefferson had boundless faith in the masses" would appear to be just a little ridiculous in the face of such assertions of his as the following: "The mobs of great cities add just so much to the support of pure government, as sores do to the strength of the human body,"[5] and, "I consider the class of artificers as the panders of vice, and the instruments by which the liberties of a country are generally overturned."[6] A boundless faith in the masses is exactly what he did not have, unless we are to suppose that the "masses" in America as late as 1800 included only "the chosen people of God who labor in the earth."[7]

Furthermore, instead of maintaining limitless confidence

[1] Richardson, *op. cit.*, vol. I, p. 322.

[2] Charles A. Beard, *The Economic Origins of Jeffersonian Democracy*, New York, 1915, p. 456.

[3] Locke, *op. cit.*, pp. 184-85.

[4] Ephraim D. Adams, *The Power of Ideals in American History*, New Haven, 1926, p. 133.

[5] *Writings of Jefferson* (Washington ed.), vol. I, p. 403.

[6] *Ibid.*, vol. I, p. 403.

[7] *Ibid.*, vol. VIII, p. 405.

in the masses, Jefferson affirmed his belief as late as 1813 in a "natural aristocracy," the foundations of which "are virtue and talent," as distinguished from an "artificial aristocracy founded on wealth and birth." He did not subscribe to the doctrine of the equality of all men except in the sense of equality before the law. He considered the natural aristocracy "the most precious gift of nature, for the instruction, the trusts, and the government of society." "May we not say," he went on to inquire, "that that form of government is the best which provides the most effectively for a pure selection of these natural aristoi into the offices of government?"[1]

If Jefferson had really believed that the cure for the evils of democracy is more democracy, he certainly would have advocated universal suffrage and direct popular election of the officers of government as absolute minimum essentials. But this was not quite the case. In 1776 he drafted a plan for a constitution of Virginia that revealed no great enthusiasm for either of these measures. The plan provided for landholding qualifications to vote for members of the lower house, at the same time recommending that the State should make grants out of the public domain to all non-landholders. Eventually this would mean universal manhood suffrage, but the enfranchised would vote not as citizens, but as property owners. The plan also provided for a senate elected by the lower house for a nine year term, an executive chosen by the same body, and judges with life tenure.[2] In 1783 he drafted another plan only slightly more democratic. It did provide for the

[1] Letter to John Adams, Oct. 28, 1813, *Writings of Jefferson* (Ford ed.), vol. IX, pp. 425-26.

[2] *Ibid.*, vol. II, pp. 7ff.

enfranchisement of all free males who possessed a amount of real property or who had served in the But it also provided for a senate elected indirect electors chosen by the people, a judiciary with life te and an executive with a veto power.[1]

In reality, Jefferson's vision of democracy was "simply a faith in personal liberty as the highest guiding principle in the progress of civilization."[2] To him the great object of government was to secure the natural rights of the individual, and certain democratic methods like popular election of the lower house of the legislature were merely the best means of realizing that object, not ends in themselves. Instead of a positive good, he conceived of government as a necessary evil, and declared that that government is best which governs least. His philosophy also embraced a demand for equal and exact justice, periodic revisions of constitutions and laws, and subordination of the military to the civil authority. Finally, it included opposition to judicial supremacy over the other branches of the government and a belief in the necessity of popular education and in the importance of local government.[3]

How closely did Madison's theory of democracy correspond with this? So far as concerns fundamentals there was substantial agreement. Both men abhorred absolutism regardless of its form. Both adhered to the ideals of limited government, dominance of the civil authority over the military, universal suffrage (in principle), and the importance of popular education and local government. Both

[1] *Works of Jefferson* (Washington ed.), vol. VIII, p. 444.

[2] Ephraim D. Adams, *op. cit.*, p. 130.

[3] *Cf.* C. E. Merriam, Jr., "The Political Theory of Jefferson," *Political Science Quarterly*, vol. XVII (March, 1902), pp. 33-39.

regarded the preservation of natural rights as the great object of political society, although Madison was more inclined than Jefferson to think of natural rights in terms of property. Both distrusted the proletarian masses of large cities, the hangers-on of parasitic capitalists, the rootless mobs that have neither the stability nor the independence essential for the responsibilities of citizenship. The chief differences in the theories of the two men would seem to consist in Madison's more cynical view of human motives, his Whiggish emphasis upon property rights, his opposition to frequent submission of constitutions and laws to the people, and his disposition at times, particularly in his earlier career, to sacrifice liberty to order. One cannot imagine Madison rejoicing over Shays' Rebellion or declaring as Jefferson did in 1789 that "The tree of liberty needs to be refreshed from time to time with the blood of patriots and tyrants."[1] After 1789, however, these divergencies in theory tended gradually to disappear, and it is not without significance that in actual political practice the policies of the two men were scarcely distinguishable, in reference to democracy as well as nearly everything else.

[1] *Writings of Jefferson* (Ford ed.), vol. IV, p. 467.

FOUR

# Republicanism

IN *Jefferson and Madison: The Great Collaboration,* Adrienne Koch wrote that both Jefferson and Madison "were staunch and far-seeing democrats in the most moral sense of the term." The former, she said, concentrated on individual rights and on striving to aid the underdog minority to become the legal majority. The latter devoted his political strength to effecting order and "a reasonable atmosphere for civilized compromise" in all the variegated affairs of state.[1] If by "the most moral sense of the term" the author meant that which is right or which ought to be, her statement with respect to Madison, at least, requires serious modification. Effecting order and promoting a reasonable atmosphere for compromise may well be admirable qualities, but they hardly entitle one to classification as a staunch democrat. The first is the mark of a conservative, while the second would befit a temporizer or opportunist better than a champion of a high ideal.

## REPUBLICANISM VERSUS DEMOCRACY

The most recent research presents Madison as fundamentally a whig or a republican rather than a democrat. This classification involves using the term whig in

[1] Adrienne Koch, *Jefferson and Madison: The Great Collaboration,* New York, 1950, pp. 293–94.

the English sense of an opponent of aristocracy, the Established Church, and the military, and a stalwart defender of property and of limited popular government. Madison qualified under all of these classifications. He despised an hereditary aristocracy, whether titled or not. He strove valiantly against an establishment of religion, as evidenced by his efforts on behalf of the First Amendment. The chief purpose of this amendment, in its final form, was to outlaw every approach to a Federal established church. It is significant that its author attempted also to make its restrictions applicable to the States, but the proposal was defeated in the Senate.[1] That Madison was a vocal defender of property can be readily demonstrated from his writings. In good Lockean fashion he invariably coupled property with liberty as the great natural rights. Yet he never espoused an unlimited right to accumulate and enjoy riches. He excoriated many times the aggressive, stock-jobbing capitalism of the money-barons of his day. The property he favored meant property in the sense of real wealth—land, buildings, money. It did not embrace "value" resulting from speculation. And it should not be unlimited. Writing in the *National Gazette* in 1792, Madison urged the enactment of laws which, while respecting the rights of property, would "reduce extreme wealth towards a state of mediocrity" and "raise extreme indigence towards a state of comfort." He was not a socialist, and he made no more than a tentative obeisance toward the welfare state. Both of these systems would

[1] Irving Brant, *James Madison,* Indianapolis, 1941–1961, vol. III, p. 273.

have violated his strong prepossessions in favor of limited government. Moreover, they would have contradicted his Malthusian conception of society, with poverty an unavoidable consequence of too rapid an increase in population. He would therefore grant the lower classes his sympathy, but he would withhold from them direct beneficence.

In Number 10 of the *Federalist* Madison defined a republic as a government extending over a considerable sphere and based upon representation, as contrasted with a pure democracy in which a small body of citizens "assemble and administer the government in person." Representation often seemed to him the very substance of free government. Its function was "to refine and enlarge the public views" by passing them through the medium of a select body of citizens whose patriotism and love of justice would rise above all "temporary and partial considerations." It might often happen, he alleged, that the popular will expressed through these representatives would be more consonant with the general good than that of the people themselves expressed directly.[1] During most stages of his career Madison profoundly distrusted the masses. In 1788 he wrote, "There can be no doubt that there are subjects to which the capacities of the bulk of mankind are unequal," and on which they must be governed by their superiors. Just twelve years before his death he pilloried the masses as the chronic victims of factious tendencies, of violent hatreds and short-sighted impulses that often lead them to impose defective and unnecessary laws that are diffi-

[1] *Federalist,* Modern Library edition, pp. 58–59.

cult to repeal even after time and reflection have shown them to be unwise.[1]

NB

Madison defined a republic also as a government deriving all its powers, directly or indirectly, from the great body of the people, "not from an inconsiderable proportion, or a favored class of it." He added that it should be administered "by persons holding their offices during pleasure, for a limited period, or during good behavior."[2] There was nothing here incompatible with a lifetime President, as advocated by Hamilton, or an appointive executive council to impose an absolute veto upon legislative enactments. To be sure, he did advocate the separation of powers, but the purpose of this was to frustrate popular sovereignty, not to ensure it. There was actually not much in Madison's concept of a republic that would prevent its being used as a model for the Gaullist regime in France or Nasser's "democracy" in the UAR. Of course, he was not seeking to promote the cause of autocracy. He hated and feared personal despotism; but he feared even more the despotism of the turbulent masses. In the Virginia ratifying convention, for example, he rejected Patrick Henry's contention that loss of liberty usually resulted from the tyranny of rulers. Far more often, he alleged, tyranny was produced by the turbulence, violence, and abuse of power exercised by the majority trampling on the rights of the minority.[3]

One of Madison's principal indictments of popular

[1] Letter to John Cartwright, 1824, *Writings* (Hunt ed.), vol. IX, pp. 181–82.

[2] *Federalist,* Modern Library edition, No. 39.

[3] Irving Brant, *op cit.,* p. 200.

government was what he regarded as its inevitable trend toward legislative predominance. He saw the legislative department as constantly striving to draw all power into its "impetuous vortex." One safeguard against this would be to divide the government into three branches—legislative, executive, and judicial—each being a check or counterweight against the others. But the separation of powers would not be sufficient. The legislative branch itself must also be divided. In addition to a popularly elected lower house, there should be a Senate constituted on an entirely different basis. Madison clearly intended that this body should be, in a sense, aristocratic—not a House of Lords, to be sure, but a body of men quite far removed from the clamoring masses. In the Philadelphia Convention he referred to symptoms of a "levelling spirit" of sufficient proportions to give notice of impending danger. How was this danger to be guarded against? Among other means, by the establishment of a body in the government sufficiently respectable for its wisdom and virtue to aid, in such emergencies, "the preponderance of justice by throwing its weight into that scale."[1] He thought its members should be chosen for long terms (nine years if possible), and that they should be sufficiently advanced in age that re-election would be a matter of little concern to them. Had he lived to the present day he would probably have been dismayed to find Senators clinging to their positions for term after term even into their seventies and eighties, partly because of the prestige of the office but mainly because of the power and

[1] Farrand, *Records of the Federal Convention*, vol. I, pp. 421–23.

perquisites accruing to them as chairmen of important committees.

According to current conceptions, democracy is almost synonymous with equal and universal suffrage, "one man, one vote." Madison had little sympathy with these conceptions. Although in the Federal Convention he did extol the right of suffrage as "an essential provision in a republican constitution," he did not intend that this right should be apportioned equally or indeed that it should be given to all. He was much too fearful of invasions of the rights of property to allow any considerable exercise of sovereignty by the multitude. Like some of his associates among the framers of the Constitution, he was apprehensive that the time would soon come when the great majority of Americans would possess neither land nor any other form of property, or, worse still, they would become the slavish dependents of industrial employers and vote not as free men but in obedience to the dictates of powerful magnates to whom they owed their livelihood.[1] It may seem incomprehensible that the leaders in the Constitutional Convention, almost without exception, should have been distrustful of the common people and oblivious of their interests. It may appear remarkable also that no one envisaged the privilege of the franchise as a basic right of citizenship essential to every man for the defense of his interests and his dignity as a person. But the truth is that the common man had no effective champion in the Convention. He was unrepresented. The majority were not fabulously rich. Some were land-poor; many were small-time lawyers or merchants who had yet to climb very

[1] *Ibid.*, vol. II, pp. 203–4.

high on the slippery ladder of economic success. But their views predominantly reflected the views of the well-to-do. Their ambitions and grievances were those of the class to which they belonged or aspired to belong. They cared very little about the rights and welfare of those below them. The great struggles within the Convention were not between rich and poor but among the owners of diverse forms of wealth. The commercial and manufacturing interests opposed each other on various issues and sometimes combined against the representatives from the small States which had no Western lands and therefore no chance of maintaining their power except through special arrangements of the governmental structure. The claims of the poor and the debtors were pushed aside by the adoption of articles against bills of credit and impairment of the obligation of contracts.

Madison's ideas on the suffrage were perhaps best summed up by two statements he made late in his life. In the Virginia Constitutional Convention of 1829 he advocated an extension of the franchise to "house keepers and heads of families." He wanted to embrace in the partnership of power every description of citizens having a sufficient stake in the public order and the stable administration of the laws; and particularly the "House keepers and Heads of families; most of whom having given hostages to fortune, will have given them to their country also." Writing about three years later, in his autobiography, he confessed that "Tho' aware of the danger of universal suffrage in a future state of Society such as the present state in Europe," he would have extended it so as to secure on every fundamental political issue a majority of people of people on the side of power. A government resting on a minority, he said, is an aristocracy, not a republic. It could never be safe with a numerical and physical force against it, "without a standing army, an enslaved press, and a disarmed populace." It is certainly apparent that neither of the standards he set up would really approximate universal suffrage. Restricting the vote to "house keepers and heads of families" and guaranteeing merely the suffrage of the majority could still exclude thousands of field hands, journeymen and industrial workers, and even adult sons of well-to-do families who did not maintain their own establishments. It may be worthy of comment that at the time Madison made these statements, several States had already adopted what practically amounted to universal manhood suffrage. They included Pennsylvania, Vermont, Maryland, Connecticut, and New York.[1]

## CONCENTRATED GOVERNMENT

Concentrated government, as distinguished from a decentralized and restricted system, is not easily reconcilable with democracy. It bears no necessary incompatibility with republicanism. At any rate, that was the conviction of Madison. He began his career as a nationalist, as opposed to a confederationist, in the movement leading to the adoption of the Constitution. According to his most eminent biographer, he remained a nationalist to the end of his life.[2] In only two important instances did he seemingly depart from his general assumption that the central government should be a gov-

[1] Charles A. Beard and Mary R. Beard, *The Rise of American Civilization,* (New York, 1927), vol. I, pp. 543–44.

[2] Irving Brant, *op cit.,* vol. III, p. 470.

ernment of preponderant authority. The first was his rejection of Hamilton's interpretation of the general welfare clause (Article I, section 8, of the Constitution). He denied that this clause had ever been intended as a grant of power. More specifically, he opposed its interpretation as an authorization of Congressional power to tax and spend for the general welfare. Under such an interpretation, he contended, national government could assume control over religion or education or any other object of State legislation down to the most trivial police measure.[1] He maintained that the delegates in the Federal Convention would have shrunk in horror from a proposal of this sort if it had ever been suggested to them. Instead, he argued, the general welfare clause crept into the Constitution as a kind of freak of history. A similar clause was contained in the Articles of Confederation and was carried over into the new Constitution as a kind of paragraph sentence or general introduction to a list of specified powers. Neither in the old instrument or in the new was it intended in itself as a grant of substantive power.[2]

By a curious contrast, Madison rejected only in part the Hamiltonian doctrine of implied powers under the necessary and proper clause. In the main he followed the Jeffersonian contention that "necessary" does not mean simply convenient for or conducive to, but really necessary. To give a loose construction to this clause, he insisted, would make it possible for Congress to exercise virtually unlimited power, in fact to do almost everything that the States could do. In the First Con-

[1] *Annals of Congress,* vol. III, pp. 387–88.

[2] *Madison Papers,* Library of Congress.

gress, apropos of a plan to establish a United States Bank, he avowed that Hamilton's means-end logic would lead to an indefinite applicability. To borrow money would be made the end and the accumulation of capital implied as the means. Then the accumulation of capital would become the end, and a Bank would be posited as the necessary means. Finally, with the Bank as the end, charters of incorporation, monopolies, and even capital punishments could be implied as means. The result would be the emergence of an all-sovereign state with no effective limitation upon its exercise of arbitrary power in any sphere.[1]

Yet a short time before Madison had written in Number 44 of the *Federalist*: "No axiom is more clearly established in law, or in reason, than that wherever the end is required, the means are authorized; wherever a general power to do a thing is given, every particular power necessary for doing it is included.[2] The resemblance between this passage and John Marshall's famous dictum in McCulloch *v.* Maryland seems closer than is commonly supposed. Furthermore, Madison, as a member of the First Congress, advocated sundry kinds of subsidies and restrictions by the Federal government. Among them were tariffs to encourage domestic manufactures, especially of those types that might otherwise have difficulty in becoming established in America; sumptuary duties to discourage luxury spending; duties to develop the means of national defense; and duties for the benefit of American shipping. He justified all of these as necessary means to the regulation of com-

[1] *Writings* (Hunt ed.), vol. VI, p. 31.

[2] *Federalist,* Modern Library edition, p. 294.

merce.[1] In 1816, near the end of his second term as President, he was able to find a United States Bank a desirable instrument for assisting Congress in the management of the nation's finances. Reversing the position he had taken twenty-four years before, he now contended that a Bank was "almost" a necessity, and that precedent and popular acceptance had sanctioned its constitutionality.[2]

The other significant example of Madison's departure from his general belief in a central government of concentrated powers was his authorship of the Virginia Resolutions. In this instance he was concerned with protecting individual liberties against the encroachments of Federal power. State sovereignty seemed to him the most effective weapon for this purpose. The Alien and Sedition Laws enacted by Congress in 1789 threatened the whole structure of fundamental rights regarded by him as the sum and substance of political freedom. In urging the States to oppose these laws he did not advocate nullification or secession or any other action by a single State in disregard of the rights and wishes of the others. What he claimed he had in mind was an invitation or recommendation by Virginia to the other States to "interpose" collectively for the purpose of curbing Federal tyranny. Such "interposition" might take the form of remonstrances, of the initiation of impeachments or amendments to the Constitution, or of appeals to the judiciary. He maintained that the Constitution was a compact among the people in the States. The State governments had had nothing to do with making

[1] *Annals of Congress,* April 8, 9, 1789.

[2] Irving Brant, *op. cit.,* vol. VI, p. 403.

it or adopting it. No one of them, therefore, could legally withdraw from the compact or nullify a law of the central government enacted under it. Only the States collectively, or at least a majority of them, could finally construe the meaning of the compact or dissolve it. Attempts by extreme defenders of States' rights in the decades before the Civil War, and in more recent times with reference to the desegregation movement, to enlist Madison on their side were based on a misinterpretation of his political theory. He repudiated the notion that the Union was a mere league of governments resting upon the prior authority of its members. On the contrary, he conceived of the United States as a true state with both the central government and the member units having sovereign powers guaranteed by the Constitution itself.

As noted already, Madison entered the Federal Convention of 1789 so convinced an advocate of a strong national government that he regarded the Articles of Confederation as hopelessly outmoded and ready to be thrown into the discard. Much earlier he had made strenuous efforts to give the government under the Articles a strong backbone of authority. In 1781 he proposed an amendment providing that if any one or more of the States should refuse or neglect to obey the United States Congress, the latter should be fully authorized to employ the forces of the United States, "by sea or by land," to compel such State or States to fulfill their Federal engagements, and "particularly to make distraint on any of the effects Vessels and Merchandizes of such state or states or of any of the citizens thereof wherever found . . ."[1] He did not seem to realize that actions of this kind taken against one or more States by a combination of other States would not be coercions of law but acts of war.

Madison did not present the famous Virginia Plan to the Constitutional Convention. The formal presentation was delegated to Edmund Randolph, who, at the time, was more powerful politically. Yet the authorship of the future President, or at least his influence, was clearly apparent.[2] The Plan provided for a strong executive and for a veto by the national legislature of all laws passed by the States. It provided also for calling forth "the force of the Union against any member failing to fulfill its duty under the Articles thereof."[3] Madison continued to advocate a Federal veto on State legislation throughout the sessions of the Convention and afterward. On October 24, 1787, in a letter to Jefferson, he recognized that the Supreme Court would be partially effective in nullifying unjust laws, but he argued that "it is more convenient to prevent the passage of a law than to void it after it is passed . . . Injustice may be effected by such an infinitude of legislative expedients, that when the disposition exists it can only be controlled by some provision which reaches all cases whatsoever." He contended that the want of such control was the besetting weakness in all ancient and modern confederacies. He did not believe that a powerful

[1] *Madison Papers* (William T. Hutchinson and William M. E. Rachal eds.), Chicago, 1962–1965, vol. III, p. 18.

[2] Irving Brant, *op. cit.*, vol. II, pp. 23–24.

[3] J. W. Pratt, "James Madison," *Dictionary of American Biography* (Dumas Malone ed.), New York, 1933, vol. XII, p. 186.

executive or even a standing army would be sufficient safeguards against the encroachments of local sovereignties. The new Constitution, he feared, made the central government too dependent on the subordinate authorities. The Senate would represent the State legislatures, the House the people of the States. Even the President would derive "his appointment from the States" and would be "periodically accountable to them."[1] This opinion contrasted rather sharply with the views he expressed later in Number 39 of the *Federalist,* contending that the new system represented a nicely adjusted balance between State and Federal principles. Despite this, his preference for strength in the national sphere seemed to predominate throughout most of his life.

Notwithstanding his nationalism, Madison continued to see enormous virtues in the federal system of divided sovereignty which he and Alexander Hamilton had largely invented. This was a system founded upon principles completely different from those of all hitherto existing confederacies. Indeed, the United States as established by the new Constitution was not a confederacy at all. It was a body politic resting upon a compact made by the people of the States in a Convention of their representatives. This compact was the Constitution of the United States, which divided the sovereign power between the central government and the subdivisions. To the former was given a grant of powers it could exercise regardless of the will of the States. The remaining components of sovereignty were reserved to the subdivisions. Most important of all, both the central and State governments acquired authority to act

[1] *Writings* (Hunt ed.), vol. V, p. 294.

directly upon individuals—to collect taxes from them, to enforce laws against them, and, at least in some limited ways, to promote their welfare. Contrary to the original recommendations of Madison, the central government received no authority to coerce or punish a State. It was not their instrument, and it was not intended to operate through them or upon them. Instead, its operation was to be restricted to individuals. They were its subjects concerning all those matters assigned to the jurisdiction of the United States. It was this vital principle which distinguished the new system from all the confederations of history. They were mere leagues of states bound together by a treaty and with a central government acting as their agent. Shortly before his death Madison envisaged this wonderful federal system of the United States as suitable for extension over the entire globe. Like John Fiske and David Starr Jordan in later times, he dreamed of the American federal system as comprehending a model for a world republic. "Nothing but time and space," he wrote, could limit its "practical extension over the globe." Any physical obstacles to unrestricted expansion would be vastly reduced by "mechanical improvements, made and to be made."[1]

## REPUBLICAN AUTOCRACY

No doubt it was inevitable that an executive so uncommanding in appearance and apparently so self-effacing as Madison should have gone down in the minds of most students of history as a weak and ineffectual President. Actually, he espoused the concept of a vigorous chief magistrate and conducted the affairs of the office

[1] Memo, *Madison Papers,* Library of Congress.

in a manner more suggestive of Andrew Jackson and Theodore Roosevelt than of George Washington or Thomas Jefferson. He was by no means the "withered little apple-john" portrayed by Washington Irving. Only when it seemed to him that executive tyranny was in the process of developing or when Congress was being pushed into the background did he lean toward restrictions on the power of the President. Such a condition arose during the rigorous enforcement of the Alien and Sedition Acts by the Adams administration. At that time Madison pointed to the danger that a multiplication of the functions of government would lead to delegation of more and more powers to the executive, while an increase in the number of offices at the disposal of the President would enable him to build a political machine and secure his indefinite continuance in office.[1] But these fears did not comport with Madison's general attitude toward executive power. He worried about legislative despotism much more than he did about that of any other branch of the government. Early in the Convention of 1787 he voted for a motion that the President hold office during good behavior.[2] In later years he condemned proposals to restrict the President's right to succeed himself and urged that he be largely exempt from legislative control in making appointments to and removals from public office. He denied that the Senate had any right to interfere with a nomination made by the President more than to accept it or to reject it. He also denied the authority of Con-

[1] Report on the Virginia Resolutions, *Writings* (Hunt ed.), vol. VI, pp. 358–59.

[2] Brant, *op. cit.*, vol. III, p. 105.

gress to limit the tenure of Presidential appointees, even to the four-year term of the President himself.[1]

But it was in the spheres of foreign and military affairs that Madison's enlargement of Presidential power received its most grandiose expression. With regard to these matters, as chief magistrate he conducted his office in a manner that was "appropriate only to an autocracy or a strong ministerial government like that of Great Britain."[2] It is certainly one of the supreme ironies of American history that the "Father of the Constitution" himself should have laid the foundations for making the President of the United States, in the conduct of foreign relations, one of the most despotic and irresponsible rulers in the world today. Madison's record of tortuous diplomacy, of distorting and falsifying facts, of withholding vital information, of misleading the public into believing that speeches and editorials written by him, or by his closest lieutenants, were really the work of others could hardly be surpassed by a Metternich or a Bismarck. Of course, he did not defend such practices in theory. He knew too much to attempt to justify them on the basis of history or abstract logic. On the contrary, his *reasoning* was generally much different. In the Constitutional Convention, for example, he avowed that "the means of defence against foreign danger have always been the instruments of tyranny at home." He called to witness the ancient Romans, among whom "it was a standing maxim to excite a war, whenever a revolt was apprehended." He thought that

[1] *Writings* (Hunt ed.), vol. V, pp. 289–90; vol. IX, pp. 43–44, 112–13.
[2] Brant, *op. cit.,* vol. VI.

the insular position of Great Britain was the principal cause of her people being less enslaved by despotic rulers bent upon using the exigencies of war to bully their subjects into subservience. This position rendered less defense necessary and "admitted a kind of defence which could not be used for the purpose of oppression."[1] As Secretary of State he affirmed the Jefferson administration's devotion to peace and laid down the theoretical principle that the executive "has no right to commit the nation to war, nor take any steps which would deprive Congress of a free choice between war and peace."[2]

His own actions, however, like those of many of his successors in high office, were singularly at variance with his rhetoric. Soon after becoming Secretary of State he informed Congress that the Floridas and New Orleans "command the only outlets to the sea" for the American West and "must become a part of the United States, either by purchase or by conquest."[3] He accepted the claim that West Florida had been a part of the Louisiana Territory and therefore had been acquired by the United States when that territory was purchased in 1803. But the records of his own Department showed that this claim was fictitious. West Florida had not been ceded by Spain to France along with Louisiana in 1800, and therefore could not have been sold to the United States by the French in 1803. Later Madison encouraged a revolution in West Florida. He promised the American leaders support and ultimate annexation to

[1] Farrand, *Records of the Federal Convention,* June 29.

[2] Brant, *op. cit.,* vol. IV, p. 264.

[3] *Annals of Congress,* Jan. 12, 1803.

the United States. In 1810 a declaration of independence was issued and Madison took formal possession of the disputed territory, thereby completing what has been called "the most disgraceful diplomatic transaction of our history."[1] The main justification offered for the transaction was that West Florida was "essential to our interests"—that is, to the interests of the Democratic-Republican party, which was coming to depend more and more for votes upon the New West.

Most of the examples of Madison's political realism—or cynicism, as it was in some cases—emerged in connection with the War of 1812. There can be little doubt that he regarded that war as a Second War for Independence. He seemed to believe that Great Britain was attempting to assign to the United States a position of no consequence in the world of nations. Worse still, in his opinion, the British were bent upon the destruction of American commerce in order to preserve a monopoly for themselves. American grievances, of course, were long standing. Jefferson had attempted to deal with them by means of an embargo. It incurred the disapproval of powerful elements in the country, however, and at the end of his administration the Embargo Act was repealed. At the beginning of Madison's first term a Non-Intercourse Act was substituted, permitting commerce with all nations except Britain and France, but authorizing the President to revive trade with either upon revocation of its restrictions against American ships. Napoleon deceived Madison into believing that the French restrictive acts, the Berlin and Milan

[1] I. J. Cox, "The American Intervention in West Florida," *American Historical Review*, vol. XVII (1911–12), p. 311.

Decrees, were in process of being revoked. Americans, generally, had little interest in the issues of the titanic struggle between France and Great Britain, but many Democratic-Republicans were pro-French in their sympathies. Actually, the French were no more respectful of American rights on the seas than were the British, but they committed fewer depredations and their attitudes showed less contempt. Besides, the British laid themselves open to greater antagonism by their alleged machinations among the Indian tribes on the American frontier, providing them with goods and weapons and inciting them to massacre white settlers. Finally, Great Britain offered a more tempting target, with her numerous ships sailing the Atlantic and her enormous territory of Canada inviting American conquest.

There is no evidence that Madison played any direct part in the movement to conquer and annex Canada, but he did almost everything else in his power to make a war with Great Britain inevitable. He evidently made up his mind quite early that military action was the only recourse for the United States to secure her rights. In the summer of 1807, when the British warship *Leopard* fired shots into the *Chesapeake* after the latter refused to give up three seamen alleged to be British deserters, he drafted a bellicose proclamation excluding British warships from American waters. He used such phrases as "avowed and insulting purpose," "lawless and bloody purpose," and "the blood of citizens wickedly shed." Unless Great Britain gave prompt satisfaction, he declared, the United States must resort to "her own means" to obtain a redress of grievances.[1]

[1] Brant, *op. cit.,* vol. IV, pp. 381–83.

Although Jefferson toned down some of these belligerent phrases, there could be no doubt of the feelings of his Secretary of State. In January 1809, he supported a move in Congress to raise an army of 50,000 volunteers to avert the danger of "a sudden attack" on the United States by either Great Britain or France. Indeed, it was argued that the conduct of both had been such that the United States herself "would be justified in proceeding to immediate hostilities."[1]

After March 4, 1809, Madison lent the full weight of the Presidency to a policy of leading the way to militant action against Great Britain. During his first month in office he sent word to the British government that adherence to the Orders in Council would mean war with the United States. As with many of his subsequent fateful actions, neither Congress nor the American people had any inkling of this step.[2] Late in 1810 he secretly notified the French government that the measures he would take in case England continued her aggressions against American commerce would "necessarily lead to war."[3] In May 1811, he ordered the frigate *President* to accost the British warship *Little Belt* with a demand that it depart immediately from New York harbor, and, in case of refusal, to open fire on it. This was a calculated risk of war—a flinging down of a challenge which, fortunately, the British government did not see fit to accept.

Madison's annual message of December 1811 was a definite harbinger of war. Though it contained some

[1] *Ibid.*, vol. V. p. 35.
[2] *Ibid.*, vol. V, p. 481.
[3] *Ibid.*, vol. V, p. 221.

suggestions of conciliation, it was really belligerent to the core. The President declared that the moment had arrived when Congress would "feel the duty of putting the United States into an armor and an attitude demanded by the crisis, and corresponding with the national spirit and expectations." He recommended enlargement of the army, enlistment of volunteers, summoning and training of the militia, and stockpiling of materials for both the army and the navy.[1] The legislative branch needed no such prodding. The new Congress, whose members took their seats in December 1811, comprised a large majority of Republicans, many of them ardent proponents of war. Their leaders included Henry Clay, John C. Calhoun, Richard M. Johnson, Felix Grundy, and Peter B. Porter. These were the so-called War Hawks, who desired a conflict with Great Britain primarily because it would create an opportunity for an enlargement of the American empire. Yet it is a mistake to conclude that Congressional War Hawks drove a reluctant President into war. The stimulus to armed conflict came just as much if not more from the Administration as from any group of saber-rattlers in Congress. In the main, perfect agreement on policy existed between the Administration and the party leaders on Capitol Hill. Indeed, some recent studies reject the whole War-Hawk theory as a species of historical mythology.[2] Like all the sub-

[1] J. D. Richardson, *Messages and Papers of the Presidents,* vol. I, p. 491.

[2] See Roger H. Brown, *The Republic in Peril,* New York, 1965, and Bradford Perkins, *The Causes of the War of 1812,* New York, 1962.

sequent wars in our history, the War of 1812 would not have occurred without the maneuvering hand and initiative of the Executive.

One of Madison's interesting devices in directing the nation along the path toward military action was his use of the *National Intelligencer* to make it appear that sentiment for war was growing rapidly outside the boundaries of the executive branch. Though privately owned, the *Intelligencer* was really the mouthpiece of the Administration. Many of its editorials were inspired, and some were actually written, by Madison himself. To illustrate, the issue of April 9, 1812, declared: "The final step ought to be taken, and that step is WAR . . . open and manly war." The impression was allowed to spread that this exhortation was written by Henry Clay, and that it represented the machinations of the War Hawks trying to push Madison into requesting a declaration of war. The truth has since been discovered that the author of the editorial was James Monroe, Madison's Secretary of State, and that it was probably written by direction of the President himself.[1]

That war between the United States and Great Britain in 1812 was unnecessary seems to be the considered judgment of most leading historians. Before the outbreak of hostilities the British had conceded many of the demands made upon them. They had agreed to repeal their Orders in Council if Napoleon would revoke his Berlin and Milan Decrees. But Madison insisted that Britain must act first. He knew that many members of his party were determined, for ex-

[1] Brant, *op. cit.*, vol. V, pp. 434–36.

pansionist reasons, to engage in an armed conflict with the British. He evidently feared that a conciliatory policy would jeopardize his party's control of Congress and probably his own chances of re-election in 1812. Indeed, the *National Intelligencer* had announced that further forbearance toward Great Britain could "scarcely fail exposing us to the imputation of pusillanimity."[1] On April 1, 1812, in a secret message to Congress, Madison asked for a sixty-day embargo against Great Britain as a "step to war."[2] He was more firmly convinced than ever that he had no alternative but to unsheathe the sword or submit. Submission, he feared, would lead to the conclusion that the Democratic-Republicans were not competent to protect the interests of the nation. As a consequence, the voters might turn the government over to the Federalists in the coming election. He had strong apprehensions, also, that the whole future of the Republic was at stake in this crisis. If it could not rise to the emergency threatening its commerce and industry, it would lose all the prestige it had gained since its founding and might well be replaced by a monarchy.[3]

### THE SANCTITY OF CIVIL LIBERTIES

In one area Madison's record of loyalty to his professions was unsurpassed and was entirely in harmony with contemporary democratic ideals. This was the field of the right and liberties of individuals. Even during the War of 1812, when dissension against his

[1] *Ibid.,* vol. V, p. 355.
[2] *Ibid.,* vol. V. p. 429.
[3] Brown, *op. cit.,* p. 14.

policies was rampant, especially in New England, he instituted no measures of censorship or stern repression against his enemies. Only one instance of contemplated arbitrary action against individuals may be regarded as an exception. In 1814, when the fortunes of war had sunk to a low ebb, he asked Congress for conscription of soldiers. He proposed that the regular army be brought up to its authorized strength of 62,448 by classifying the militia and subjecting it to a draft.[1]

The freedoms now often assigned the preferred position among the guaranties of the Bill of Rights are the freedoms of the First Amendment. Heading the list is that pertaining to religion. Congress is forbidden to make any law "respecting an establishment of religion, or prohibiting the free exercise thereof." As we have seen, Madison was largely responsible for the final form that this amendment took. Whether he actually meant it as a guaranty of the complete freedom of the individual to believe or disbelieve whatever he chose regarding religion is not certain. He referred, in the Virginia ratifying convention, to a belief in God as "essential to the moral order of the world and to the happiness of man."[2] But there can be no doubt that he severely reprobated any attempt on the part of the state to give preference to one religion over another, or to give aid or support to any religion no matter how orthodox its adherents conceived it to be. When barely two years out of Princeton, he wrote to his friend William Bradford that if the Church of England had been the "established and general Religion in the

[1] Brant, *op. cit.*, vol. VI, p. 337.

[2] Elliot, *Debates*, vol. III, p. 330.

colonies," slavery and subjection "would have been gradually insinuated among us." "Ecclesiastical Establishments," he went on, "tend to great ignorance and corruption, all of which facilitate the Execution of mischievous Projects."[1] In 1785, as a member of the Virginia House of Delegates, he vehemently opposed a bill introduced by Patrick Henry levying a general tax for the support of "teachers of the Christian Religion." Such an aid to religion, he declared, would differ only in degree from the Inquisition. "The one is the first step, the other the last, in the career of intolerance."[2]

Madison's official acts pertaining to religion conformed to his theoretical views. He insisted upon the absolute exemption of religion from control, assistance, or restriction by the state. More than once he condemned the doctrine that some alliance or coalition between church and state is necessary for the health of both. Toward the end of his public career, he disapproved of the appointment of chaplains to be paid out of the public treasury, suggesting that if any legislator felt that he needed the ministrations of one of these, he should obtain their services at his own expense. Finally, in issuing Thanksgiving proclamations, President Madison merely "invited" those who were "piously disposed" to give thanks and offer supplications to the "Great Parent and Sovereign of the Universe." He did not "recommend" or "call upon."[3] It would have redounded even more to his credit if he had urged with greater emphasis that a man's religious beliefs

[1] *Madison Papers* (University of Chicago ed.), vol. I, p. 105.

[2] *Writings* (Cong. ed.), vol. I, p. 166.

[3] Brant, *op. cit.*, vol. VI, p. 198.

are an exclusively private matter and that freedom of conscience admits of no interference. He could have given the First Amendment added value if he had insisted that it read: "Congress shall make no law respecting an establishment of religion or infringing the rights of conscience." In one of the earlier drafts approved by Madison, it did contain a freedom of conscience phrase, but he allowed it to be stricken out in order to obtain unanimous support.[1]

Madison's doctrine of freedom of speech and of the press was as absolute and unequivocal as that of Justice Hugo L. Black in our own day. Indeed, the renowned justice has on more than one occasion cited Madison's views as a basis for his own interpretation of the First Amendment.[2] The Father of the Constitution made his most vigorous assertions on freedom of expression in condemning the Sedition Act of 1798. He characterized the prohibitions laid upon Congress by the First Amendment as unexceptionable. He denied the possibility of drawing a distinction between freedom and "licentiousness," especially of the press. No means have ever yet been devised, he insisted, by which the press can be corrected without being enslaved. A supposed freedom which admits of exceptions, alleged to be dangerous and irresponsible, is not freedom at all. He maintained this position throughout the most critical days of his career. As already mentioned, during the darkest days of the War of 1812 he took no steps to curb the freedom of those who were against him. He remained

[1] *Ibid.,* vol. III, p. 271.

[2] Yates *v.* United States, 354 U.S. 343; Beauharnais *v.* Illinois, 343 U.S. 250.

steadfast no matter how vile the calumnies showered upon him, even when other leaders of his party were clamoring for "tar and feathers, hemp and confiscation."[1] His stand in this regard was his most creditable act in a misguided and blundering administration.

[1] Brant, *op. cit.*, vol. VI, p. 32.

FIVE

# Theory of the Union and the Constitution

## THE UNIQUE CHARACTER OF THE UNION AND THE CONSTITUTION

AS I attempted to show in Chapter Two, Madison did not conceive of the state as organic, as a product of history or evolution. According to his way of thinking, every political society is created by the voluntary act of its own members. In other words, the state has no other basis than compact or agreement. The parties to the compact may be either individuals or communities; but, whichever they are, until they definitely agree to become one society, they are merely so many atoms, as discrete as the individual pebbles in a heap of gravel. No factors of geography or race or history can suffice to make them a state.

Holding to such a view as this, Madison could not regard the American Union as older than the Constitution or the States. He could not conceive of the Union as having been in any sense produced by the unfoldment of some national destiny in the events of the Revolution or in the organization of the First and Second Continental Congresses and the establishment of the Confederation.[1] It

[1] Origin of the Constitutional Convention, *Writings* (Hunt. ed.), vol. II, pp. 392-96.

remained for Webster to make this "discovery" many years later. To be sure Madison recognized that a kind of imperfect union of the States had existed under the Articles of Confederation, but he maintained that it was not a true state. The Articles were not a compact analogous to the fundamental compact by which a state is formed and in which the majority has an indefinite right to bind the whole. On the contrary they were analogous to a convention or a treaty among individual states.[1] Besides, this imperfect union was not the one that exists now. The union under the Articles was supplanted in 1789 by a new Union, a true state with a government of sovereign powers, and not a mere confederation.[2]

In Madison's view nothing seemed clearer than the idea that the Constitution was a compact. It was the agreement by which the Union of the States was "ratified," and the government of the United States organized and established.[3] This compact was unique in the manner of its formation. The original parties to it were not the people as one body acting by numerical majority, and not the State governments, but the people in each of the States in their highest sovereign capacity.[4] In other words, the Union and the Constitution were created simultaneously by a definitive agreement among sovereign communities, each stipulating with the others the conditions of union and the surrender of powers to a central government.[5]

[1] Farrand, *Records of the Federal Convention*, vol. I, p. 315.

[2] Letter to Edward Everett, Aug. 28, 1830, *Writings* (Hunt ed.), vol. IX, p. 388.

[3] Manuscript, *Madison Papers*, Library of Congress.

[4] Letter to Edward Everett, Aug. 28, 1830, *Writings* (Hunt ed.), vol. IX, p. 386.

[5] Letter to Spencer Roane, June 29, 1821, *Writings* (Hunt ed.), vol. IX, p. 66; *Federalist* (Lodge ed.), No. 39, p. 236.

The people within each State in their sovereign capacity agreed with the people in every other State to form a Union and a Constitution for the common safety and the preservation of justice among themselves in exactly the same way as individuals might form a consolidated state for similar purposes.[1]

But the Constitution of the United States is not merely a compact; according to Madison it is also a law. It was partly in order to give it this character that he insisted that it should be ratified by conventions elected by the people, and not by the State legislatures. If it were ratified by their own governments, the States would come to look upon it as a mere treaty; and a breach of it by any one of them would be held to absolve the others from their whole obligation. As a result the nation would be no whit better off than under the Articles of Confederation. But ratification by the people, the highest sovereign authority in any country, would give to the Constitution a superior sanction, and the courts would be obliged to enforce it as the supreme law of the land.[2] This conception of a constitution as a law unalterable and unassailable by a majority of the legislature, and enforceable by the courts, was a distinctively American idea.[3] It was an idea that had been well received in minds other than Madison's, for it was embodied in the Constitution of the United States with no opposition from any source in the Federal Convention.

[1] Origin of the Constitutional Convention, *Writings* (Hunt ed.), vol. II, p. 391.

[2] Farrand, *Records of the Federal Convention*, vol. I, pp. 122-23; vol. II, pp. 92-93.

[3] Charles Warren, *Congress, the Constitution and the Supreme Court*, Boston, 1930, pp. 12-16.

Madison contended that the Constitution of the United States has a character all its own. He denied that any other organic law can furnish a model for analysis or criticism of it. In the first place every other constitution has been founded upon the doctrine of indivisible sovereignty; whereas the Constitution of the United States divides the sovereignty between local governments and a central government. The latter is no less a government within the sphere of its powers than are the former within their several spheres. Like them it operates directly on persons and things and has at its command a physical force for executing the powers committed to it.[1] Madison scoffed at the idea that sovereignty cannot be divided or alienated. That would only be the case, he maintained, if the division or cession were not mutual and equal, but when there is both mutuality and equality there is no real sacrifice on either side; what one grants the other gains. It is on this principle that treaties, by which rights are granted at the expense of internal authority, are not considered inconsistent with the sovereignty of the parties to them.[2] He insisted that, in practice, divisions of sovereignty are actually made, and everyone takes them for granted. The separations of Maine from Massachusetts and Kentucky from Virginia were certainly cases in point. If one State could alienate a portion of its territory so as to create a new sovereignty, why could not a number of States effect their incorporation into a new sovereignty by a partial surrender, not of terri-

[1] Letter to Edward Everett, Aug. 28, 1830, *Writings* (Hunt ed.), vol. IX, p. 388.

[2] Letter to Robert Y. Hayne, April, 1830, *Writings* (Hunt ed.), vol. IX, pp. 390-91.

tory or of population, but merely of certain ultimate powers belonging to themselves?[1]

In the second place every other constitution that the world has known has provided, according to Madison, for either a national government or a league of governments. The Constitution of the United States, however, is neither national nor federal, but a composition of both. It will be noted that Madison was not using the word "federal" in quite the sense of confederate, for he was thinking in terms of the people in the States as sovereign communities, rather than of State governments. So far as concerns its foundation, the Constitution is a federal instrument, he pointed out, since it provides for ratification by the people, not as individuals composing one nation, but as citizens of their respective States. In respect of the derivation of powers it provides for a system partly national and partly federal. The House of Representatives is appointed by the people in their individual capacities. To that extent the government is national. The Senate, on the other hand, rests upon the States as co-equal societies, thereby suggesting a federal character. The executive power is derived from a composite source. The choice of electors is to be made, first of all, by the States in their political characters, but the States are allotted votes in the Electoral College partly on the basis of their being co-ordinate political units, and partly on the basis of their being unequal members of one society.[2]

With regard to the operation of the government the Constitution is undoubtedly national, he explained, in that the government operates directly upon individuals; whereas

[1] Sovereignty, *Writings* (Hunt ed.), vol. IX, p. 571.

[2] *Federalist* (Lodge ed.), No. 39, pp. 236-37.

under a federal instrument it would operate on the several political units composing the Union. But the *extent* of the government's powers under the Constitution presents a different case. If it were a national Constitution, the general government would be given an indefinite authority over all persons and things within the territory of the Union. The units of local government would have only such powers as the general government might suffer them to exercise. Its supremacy over these units would be complete: it could control or abolish them at its pleasure. That the Constitution has a distinctly federal character is amply attested by the fact that it gives to the general government jurisdiction over certain enumerated objects only, leaving to the States "a residual and inviolable sovereignty over all other objects." It is true, he admitted, that any questions of a conflict between the two jurisdictions are to be decided by a tribunal of the general government; but this does not vitiate the federal principle, for the decisions will have to be made impartially in accordance with the rules of the Constitution.[1]

In relation to the amending process the Constitution represents again, according to Madison, a combination of the federal and national characters. In permitting proposed amendments to be adopted by less than a unanimous vote of the States, it partakes of a national character. In requiring the concurrence of more than a majority of them, however, "and particularly in computing the proportion by *States*, not by *citizens*," it substitutes the federal for the national principle.[2]

Madison's ideal, then, was a Constitution which was both

[1] *Ibid.*, No. 39, p. 238.
[2] *Ibid.*, No. 39, p. 239.

a compact and a law and an expression of the will of the people in dividing sovereign powers between central and local authorities. He hoped the division that had been made would establish a just equilibrium of the two and not a preponderance of either the one or the other. Nevertheless, he himself really made the Constitution a compact among the States and regarded their very existence as an automatic limitation on the general government.[1] Moreover, in the First Congress he declared that the powers not delegated by the Constitution, nor prohibited by it to the States, "are reserved to the States respectively"—not to the people of the nation as a whole.[2] He seemed to have only a vague perception of the forces making for national dominance and the destruction of States' rights. He recognized that a substantial increase in the number of States and the presence of an external danger would be likely to strengthen the general government at the expense of the States,[3] but he overlooked other factors making for the same result, among them the rapid growth of the North in comparison with the South, the weakening of the old local attachments with the expansion of population into the Western country, the improvement of transportation facilities, and, most of all, the development of a more complex economic life. By a curious irony of fate he himself contributed about as much as anyone to the centralizing tendency. No man did more to encourage westward expansionism; or, with the exception of Hamilton, to foster the growth of industrialism in the North.

[1] E. S. Corwin, *The Twilight of the Supreme Court*, New Haven, 1934, p. 10.

[2] *Annals of Congress*, vol. I, pp. 433, 436.

[3] Letter to John G. Jackson, *Writings* (Hunt ed.), vol. IX, p. 76.

But of course the motives he avowed were always in harmony with his constitutional principles. For instance, he did not recommend the encouragement of manufactures in order to bestow additional power upon the central government, but rather to secure a more balanced economic life for the nation, and thereby to prevent sectional discord that might easily lead to usurpation of powers by the general government.

At one stage in his career Madison appeared to take a rather strong nationalist position. As a member of the Confederation Congress he urged various measures for increasing the powers of the central government, including a plan of taxation with revenue laws that would operate on individuals and would be exempt from State control.[1] He even insisted that the acts of the Confederation Congress were not mere recommendations but laws with as much binding effect upon the States as the acts of the latter had upon their individual citizens.[2]

It was in the Federal Convention of 1787 that Madison's nationalism received its fullest expression—in such measure that some of the extreme States' rights leaders denounced him in later years as a blatant consolidationist who had tried to reduce the States to mere provinces. Some of his statements in the Convention and in his correspondence of the time appeared to lend color to this charge. He avowed, for example, that the difficulties and dangers to which the States were subject would diminish in direct proportion to their surrender of sovereignty. The true wisdom of the small States especially, he thought, would consist in promoting a system which "would most approxi-

[1] *Writings* (Gilpin ed.), vol. I, pp. 111-12.
[2] *Ibid.*, vol. I, pp. 352-53.

mate the States to the condition of counties."[1] On another occasion he declared that if it were practicable for the general government to extend its care to every requisite object of local concern, no great calamity would result from absorption of the States by the national government. The people would not have less liberty under one great republic than under thirteen small ones.[2] One of his favorite projects was for a national veto power over State laws, to be vested either in the President or in Congress. He considered such an arrangement "absolutely necessary to a perfect system." The States, he maintained, would always be controlled by a propensity to pursue their particular interests to the disadvantage of the general interest, to encroach upon the national authority, to violate treaties, and "to oppress the weaker party within their respective jurisdictions." A national veto power would be "the great pervading principle that would control the centrifugal tendency of the States," and keep them from flying out of their proper orbits and destroying the order and harmony of the system.[3]

Even after the Convention had adjourned, Madison continued to express what appeared to be a nationalist bias. In a letter to Jefferson in October, 1787, he complained that the general government under the new Constitution was too completely derived from the local authorities. The Senate, he pointed out, would represent the States in their political character. The President would derive his appointment from the States and would be periodically ac-

[1] Farrand, *Records of the Federal Convention*, vol. I, p. 449.

[2] *Ibid.*, vol. I, pp. 357-58.

[3] *Ibid.*, vol. I, pp. 164-65; letter to Jefferson, March 19, 1787, *Writings* (Hunt ed.), vol. II, pp. 326-27.

countable to them. He did not think that the establishment of a national judiciary would be an adequate safeguard against the aggressions and injustice of the States. An individual who had been made the victim of State tyranny might not have the means to carry an appeal to the Federal Supreme Court. Furthermore, the national government itself would have no adequate protection, for a State which would trespass by legislative action upon the Federal authority would scarcely hesitate to defy the national judiciary.[1] In the *Federalist* Madison persistently denied that the framers of the Constitution had made any serious inroads upon the sovereignty of the States, but he seemed at times to imply that even if they had, such action would have been justifiable, for the condition of the country was so critical that they would have been recreant to their patriotic duty and to the confidence placed in them if they had shown a disposition to sacrifice substance to form.[2]

On the other hand, there is plenty of evidence to show that Madison was not so ardent a champion of concentrated government as the foregoing statements might indicate. Before the Convention even met he announced his opposition to any plan that would consolidate the States into one sovereignty.[3] In the Convention itself he declared that the rights of the States must be preserved "as carefully as trials by jury."[4] Late in his life he denied that his advocacy of a national power to negative State laws had sprung from any desire to establish a unitary government.

[1] *Writings* (Hunt ed.), vol. V, pp. 23-28.

[2] Lodge edition, No. 40, pp. 245-47.

[3] Letter to Edmund Randolph, *Writings* (Hunt ed.), vol. II, p. 338.

[4] Farrand, *Records of the Federal Convention*, vol. I, p. 490.

He said that he had intended this veto power to apply only to objects necessary to preserve the equilibrium of the federal system, that it should operate on essentially the same principle as the judicial veto which was later adopted as more expedient.[1] He insisted also that his use of the term "national" in the Philadelphia Convention had been solely for the purpose of distinguishing the new government from the Confederation, that it was not meant to express the extent of power of the general government but the manner of its operation, which was to be on individuals and not on States. It did not imply any purpose of consolidating the States into one aggregate sovereignty.[2]

Madison's apparent bias in favor of a strong national government during the period of the adoption of the Constitution is not hard to understand in view of the condition of the country as he saw it at the time. There were three principal evils which he was especially anxious to correct, although he seems to have exaggerated their seriousness. One was the invasion of private rights by the State legislatures, which he believed could be remedied only by some kind of effective veto power by the general government over State laws. A second was the inability of the Confederation to provide for the regulation of commerce, to prevent jealousies among the States, and to protect them against foreign danger and internal disorder. But the most serious of all was the dependence of the general government under the Articles of Confederation upon the local sovereignties, without power to enforce its

[1] Letter to N. P. Trist, Dec., 1831, *Writings* (Hunt ed.), vol. IX, p. 473; letter to John Tyler, 1833, *Writings* (Hunt ed.), vol. IX, pp. 505-6.

[2] *Ibid.*, vol. IX, p. 508.

will upon individual citizens. This confederate principle that made the States and not individuals the subjects of the general government was, according to Madison, fraught with enormous possibility of danger; for, if the government should at any time attempt to coerce its subjects, civil war would be the certain result.[1] Even without coercion the results would be almost as bad, for communities, like individuals, will disregard their obligations just in the proportion that they know there is no energy in the laws to compel fulfillment.[2]

Obviously the correction of these evils, real or alleged, necessitated some radical changes in the political system, indeed an actual revolution to abolish the confederate system entirely. That such a revolution had been accomplished with the adoption of the new Constitution was the prevailing view in the minds of leading Americans at the time,[3] including Madison himself as he rather plainly indicated in *Federalist* Number 40. The effect of this revolution, however, according to the view of the fathers, was not to abolish the sovereignty of the States, but merely to make a *division* of sovereignty between the States and the central government. In other words, the people in the States, the only true sovereigns since the establishment of independence, contracted among themselves to form a new political society, the Union, and to surrender permanently a portion of their sovereignty to the government of that Union. As a result of this division of sovereignty the new central authority received much more extensive pre-

[1] Elliott, *Debates*, vol. II, p. 200.

[2] *Ibid.*, vol. II, p. 199.

[3] E. S. Corwin, *The Doctrine of Judicial Review*, Princeton, 1914, p. 84.

rogatives than the Confederation government had ever enjoyed; but nothing like a consolidation of the country into a national unit occurred, for the states in their political character still retained the bulk of powers.

At the time the Constitution was adopted, Madison did not believe that the States were in any danger of being swallowed up in the nation. In fact he considered the real danger to be just the reverse, that the State governments would tend to absorb the general government. Here we perceive another reason that helps to account for what seemed to be his nationalist bias. He had seen the old Confederate government frequently baffled and frustrated by the stubborn independence of the States, and he was anxious to avoid this at all costs under the new system. In striving to attain such a result it was probably inevitable that he should have leaned too far in the direction of national supremacy. He seemed to think that in almost any kind of federal structure the particular units would possess the advantage and would constantly tend to encroach upon the sphere of the central authority. The total number of their employees would always exceed the number of persons employed by the central government. Their powers would be of more immediate concern to the citizens, and, anyway, the primary and natural attachment of the people is to their local governments. Moreover, under the Constitution of the United States the Federal government is made to depend in part for its very existence upon the States. And the powers given to the former are few and defined, while those reserved by the latter are numerous and indefinite.[1]

[1] *Federalist* (Lodge ed.), No. 45, pp. 288-89; Elliott, *Debates*, vol. II, pp. 203-5.

THEORY OF CONSTITUTIONAL CONSTRUCTION

Madison's conception of the foundation of the Constitution virtually necessitated a theory of strict construction of that instrument. He believed that in adopting the constitutional compact the people in the States divided the sovereignty that they possessed. Since sovereignty in its entirety has no precise limits, this division could have been made in only one of two ways. Either the people in the States must have allotted to themselves a few specific powers, leaving the undefined remainder to the general government; or else they must have made the general government a government of enumerated powers with all the rest of the sovereignty reserved to the States. That the division was not made in the former mode, he maintained, is perfectly obvious from the Constitution itself, for the powers granted to Congress are specifically enumerated. It follows that the general government can exercise only those powers that are actually granted to it, and such others as may be absolutely necessary to carry them into execution. This was the theory which Madison adhered to throughout his life as we shall see from a discussion of his doctrines of inherent powers, the necessary and proper clause, the general welfare clause, and the power to enact protective tariffs. Although he allowed to the general government several prerogatives which other strict constructionists like John Taylor would never have tolerated, he always insisted that he was not doing violence to his theory, that these powers were really conferred upon Congress either directly or by necessary implication.

He seemed anxious, however, especially in his later years, to avoid a position too rigidly doctrinaire. He suggested that in extremely doubtful cases involving the division of powers the line might be drawn in such a way that what could best be done by each government should be left for each to do: the general government to do what the local governments could not separately accomplish, or would be most likely to abuse in doing, and vice versa. In other very special cases he thought a different device might be attempted in order to render the political system competent to all the crises and advantages of government. For certain objects like a tax on exports or for needed internal improvements beyond the constitutional powers of the Federal government or the financial powers of the local authorities, he intimated that the Federal and State governments might be brought into joint action under a scheme requiring the concurrence of a certain proportion of the State legislatures with the national legislature.[1] He denied that the assent of particular States alone could confer upon Congress authority to provide for internal improvements, since this power was not granted in the Constitution.[2] His attitude toward the question of a United States Bank illustrates pretty well his ability to get away from a strictly legalistic view of constitutional construction. In spite of his savage attacks on the institution as a member of the First Congress, as President he discovered that a Bank of the United States would not be unconstitutional after all. He considered the question of constitutionality to have been settled by repeated recognitions of the validity of such an institution in

[1] Manuscript, *Madison Papers*, Library of Congress.

[2] Veto message, March 3, 1817, Richardson, *op. cit.*, vol. I, p. 585.

acts of all three branches of the government and by indications of a concurrence of the general will of the nation.[1] It is of course possible that the vital need for a Bank to rescue the country from the financial chaos of the War of 1812 aided him in making this discovery.

Madison denied that the Federal government under the Constitution of the United States has any inherent powers, that is, powers supposed to be derived from the fact of sovereignty and inferred from the general nature of government. The whole doctrine of inherent powers, he maintained, is a dangerous one not to be tolerated. He pointed out that if it had been intended to allow Congress powers derived from such a source, the entire process of defining powers would have been superfluous. Powers alleged to be inherent, he insisted, will be indefinitely multiplied by ambition and interest until the sovereignty of the States becomes a mere shadow. No other basis of division of authority save that of enumerated and reserved powers can safeguard the rights of the States against annihilation.[2] He denied that the government of the United States has any inherent power of self-preservation entitling it to do whatever it may judge necessary for that purpose.[3] However essential to the nature of government a particular power may be, it is not the property of the Federal government in this country unless it is granted or necessarily implied in the Constitution. Had the power of making treaties, for example, been omitted, "the defect

[1] *Ibid.*, vol. I, p. 555.

[2] Address of the General Assembly to the People of the Commonwealth of Virginia, January, 1799, *Writings* (Hunt ed.), vol. VI, p. 335.

[3] *Ibid.*, vol. VI, p. 335.

could only have been lamented, or supplied by an amendment of the Constitution."[1]

In similar fashion Madison denied that the Federal government derives any authority from a supposed common law of the United States. He rejected the notion that there had ever been such a law pervading and operating through the whole country as one society. He admitted that before the Revolution the English common law, under various limitations, formed a part of the colonial codes; but he insisted that it was a separate law for each colony within its respective limits and was not the same for any two of them. After the colonies won their independence, the common law remained in the form of different varieties of State law. It was never established as a national law either by the Articles of Confederation or by the Constitution of 1787.[2] Madison was particularly concerned with disproving that the Federal government had any common law right to abridge freedom of the press; but the issue in his judgment had a broader significance. If a common law of the United States existed as a reservoir of authority for the national government, Congress would have a very extensive police power, and the reserved powers of the States would be greatly reduced.

Madison did not insist that every power not specifically granted by the Constitution to the Federal government must be regarded as prohibited to it. If that were true many of the granted powers would be left without the necessary and proper means for carrying them into execution. In Congress he condemned a proposal to insert the

[1] *Annals of Congress*, vol. II, p. 1900.

[2] Report on the Virginia Resolutions, *Writings* (Hunt ed.), vol. VI, pp. 372-79.

word "expressly" before the word "delegated" in the Tenth Amendment, so as to make it read: "The powers not expressly delegated to the United States by the Constitution, nor prohibited by it to the States, are reserved to the States respectively, or to the people."[1] He contended that powers by implication must necessarily be admitted, declaring, for example, that Congress must be considered to have authority to encourage shipbuilding and navigation and to retaliate against trade restrictions of other countries as necessary means of regulating foreign commerce.[2]

Nevertheless, he did not mean that a loose construction should be placed on that clause of the Constitution which provides that Congress shall have power to make all laws necessary and proper for carrying into execution the enumerated powers.[3] For the most part he followed Jefferson on this question, particularly in his attack in Congress on the United States Bank. He took the stand that "necessary" does not mean simply convenient or conducive to, but really necessary. To construe it otherwise would be to destroy the essential character of the Federal government, a government of limited and enumerated powers. To give a loose construction to this clause, he insisted, would make it possible for Congress to exercise virtually unlimited powers, in fact to do almost everything that the States can do. If, for example, the establishment of a Bank is necessary to the exercise of the power to borrow money, then Congress also has the power to create the ability to lend; in other words, to charter corporations, to establish monopolies, to give bounties, and to make

[1] *Annals of Congress*, vol. I, p. 761.

[2] Letter to Professor Davis, 1832, *Writings* (Cong. ed.), vol. IV, pp. 241-42.

[3] Art. I, sec. 8, cl. 18.

regulations on every object pertaining to the general wealth or the prosperity of agriculture, commerce, and manufacturing. Such was patently not the intent of the authors of the Constitution, as other provisions of that document show. Congress is given power to regulate the value of money; yet it is expressly added, not left to implication, that counterfeiters may be punished. Armies are more incident to the power to declare war than banks are to borrowing; yet the power to raise and support armies is expressly provided for. The regulation and calling forth of the militia are directly related to the war power; yet they are not left to be discovered by logical deduction. These examples as well as others that might be pointed out "condemn the exercise of any power, particularly a great and important power, which is not evidently and necessarily involved in an express power."[1]

The decision of the Supreme Court in the case of McCulloch *v.* Maryland in 1819 gave Madison another opportunity for condemnation of loose construction of the necessary and proper clause. He could not accept for a minute Chief Justice Marshall's famous dictum: "Let the end be legitimate, let it be within the scope of the Constitution, and all means which are appropriate, which are plainly adapted to that end, which are not prohibited, but consist with the letter and spirit of the Constitution, are constitutional."[2] He feared that the application of such a principle would destroy the federal system. If all that is necessary is that the means be conducive to, or appropriate for, some legitimate end, and not expressly prohibited, then there is practically no limit to the exercise of national power, and the reserved powers of the States

[1] *Annals of Congress*, vol. II, pp. 1897-1901.

[2] 4 Wheaton 316.

become a nullity. There is hardly any conceivable act of Congress which could not be considered an appropriate means adapted to some purpose provided for in the Constitution. He pointed out further, what was undoubtedly true, that if any avowal of such a sweeping interpretation had been made at the time the Constitution was in the hands of the State conventions, the cause of ratification would have been rendered hopeless.[1]

Madison would not even admit that the necessary and proper clause could be made to justify Federal expenditures for internal improvements—unless we can find an exception in certain of his statements in the *Federalist*. In Number 42 of that series he wrote: "The power of establishing post roads must in every view be a harmless power, and may perhaps by judicious management become productive of great public conveniency. Nothing which tends to facilitate the intercourse between the States can be deemed unworthy of the public care."[2] But if he intended to imply by these assertions anything more than a Federal power to provide for the transmission of the mails, he changed his mind later on; for as President he denied that Congress had any authority to appropriate money for roads and canals save those having a bona fide postal or military object.[3] Ardently as he desired a national network of

[1] Letter to Spencer Roane, Sept. 2, 1819, *Writings* (Hunt ed.), vol. VIII, pp. 448-50.

[2] Lodge edition, pp. 266-67.

[3] Richardson, *op. cit.*, vol. I, p. 585. Jefferson took an even more extreme position than this, at least in his early career. He doubted that the power to *establish* post roads conferred any power to *make* roads, but probably only the power to select from those already made the ones on which there should be a post. Letter to Madison, March 6, 1796, *Writings of Jefferson* (Ford ed.), vol. VII, pp. 63-64.

communications, he insisted that only a constitutional amendment, or some adequate substitute therefor, could give Congress the power to provide for them.[1] It is rather difficult, though, to see why he could not have found about as much constitutional warrant for internal improvements as for the seizure of West Florida, which appeared not to trouble his political conscience in the slightest.

If Madison refused to countenance a loose construction of the necessary and proper clause, even less did he approve of a liberal interpretation of the general welfare clause. The insertion of the words "common defense and general welfare" in Article I, section 8, of the Constitution, so as to provide that "The Congress shall have power to lay and collect taxes, duties, imposts, and excises, to pay the debts and provide for the common defense and general welfare of the United States" was the result, he maintained, of a kind of freak of history. The taxing power clause as it originally stood expressed simply a power "to lay taxes, duties, imposts, and excises" without indicating any objects, and of course intended that the revenues derived should be applicable to the other specified powers of Congress. A solicitude to prevent any possible danger to the validity of the debts contracted by the Confederation led the Convention to add the phrase, "to pay the debts of the United States." Then, inasmuch as this might be taken to limit the taxing power to a single object, a familiar phrase of the Articles of Confederation, "to provide for the common defense and the general welfare," was annexed, but without any purpose of giving additional power to Congress.[2] In the new instrument as in the old this

[1] Richardson, *op. cit.*, vol. I, p. 585.

[2] Manuscript, *Madison Papers*, Library of Congress.

phrase was intended merely as a general and introductory statement to be qualified by the specific grants of power contained elsewhere.

Furthermore, according to Madison, not a single reference was ever made in the Convention to the general welfare clause as a grant of power, unless a proposal offered on the twenty-fifth of August should be considered as such. An amendment was introduced on that day to give Congress power to provide for payment of the public debts, "and for defraying the expenses that shall be incurred for the common defense and general welfare." The amendment was rejected, only one State voting for it. It is impossible to believe, Madison insisted, that the jealous defenders of States' rights in the Convention and the advocates of a strict limitation of Federal powers should have silently permitted the introduction of a phrase nullifying the very restrictions they demanded. The only explanation that is in any degree plausible, he maintained, is that the words "common defense and general welfare" were taken for granted as harmless since they were being used in precisely the same way as in the Articles of Confederation.[1]

Madison pointed out also that when the Constitution was submitted for ratification, a majority of the States proposed amendments to safeguard their own rights and the liberties of their people. Thirty-three were demanded by New York, twenty-six by North Carolina, twenty by Virginia, and smaller numbers by the others—all of them designed to circumscribe the powers of the Federal government by restrictions, explanations, and prohibitions. Yet

[1] Letter to Andrew Stevenson, Nov. 27, 1830, *Writings* (Hunt ed.), vol. IX, pp. 416-22.

not a single one of these amendments referred to the words "general welfare," which, if understood to convey a substantive power, would have been more dangerous than all of the other powers objected to combined. That the terms with any such meaning attached to them could have passed unnoticed by the State conventions, characterized as they were by strong suspicions against the whole project of a national government, was more than Madison could believe, and he did not see how anyone else could believe it.[1]

In view of these facts of history Madison argued that only one conclusion was possible, namely, that the general welfare clause was never intended to be a grant of power. Its meaning, he insisted, must be sought in the succeeding enumeration of powers, or else the general government of this country is a government without any limits whatever. If Congress as the supreme and sole judge of that subject can apply money to the general welfare, then it may assume control over religion or education or any other object of State legislation down to the most trivial police measure.[2] The only correct interpretation is to permit taxation for some particular purpose embraced within one of the enumerated powers and conducive to the general welfare. If a proposal for collecting and expending Federal revenues meets these qualifications, it is constitutional; otherwise it is not. Acceptance of the opposite interpretation would destroy the import and effect of the enumeration of powers. For, he declared, it must be patent to anyone who chooses to think on the subject that there is not a single power which may not be considered as re-

[1] *Ibid.*, vol. IX, p. 422.

[2] *Annals of Congress*, vol. III, pp. 387-88.

lated to the common defense or the general welfare; nor a power of any consequence which does not involve, or make possible, an expenditure of money. A government, therefore, which enjoyed the right to exercise power in either one or both of these premises would not be the limited government contemplated by the fathers of the Constitution, but a consolidated government of absolute power.[1]

When he came to the subject of protective tariffs, Madison seemed to waver a bit as a strict constructionist. To be sure he always maintained that the tariff power was a necessary derivative of the authority to regulate foreign commerce, but he came perilously close at times to asserting an inherent power of the Federal government to foster and protect the economic interests of the country. For example, he argued that the right to protect its manufacturing, commercial, and agricultural interests against discriminating policies of other countries belongs to every nation. Previous to the adoption of the Constitution this right existed in the governments of the individual States. The want of such an authority in the central government was deeply felt and deplored, and to supply that want was one of the chief purposes of the establishment of the new system. If the power was not transferred, then it no longer exists anywhere; for obviously it could not now be exercised by the States.[2] He contended that sovereign powers in the United States, although divided between the States in their united capacity and in their individual capacities, must nevertheless be equal to all the objects of govern-

[1] Report on the Virginia Resolutions, *Writings* (Hunt ed.), vol. VI, pp. 355-57; *Federalist* (Lodge ed.), No. 41, pp. 257-58.

[2] Notes on the Tariff, *Writings* (Hunt ed.), vol. IX, p. 323 note.

ment, except those prohibited for special reasons, such as duties on exports, and those inconsistent with the principles of republicanism.[1] Why this doctrine could not also have been applied to other powers, for example the power to construct internal improvements beyond the capacity or jurisdiction of the States, is certainly not readily apparent.

On various occasions Madison submitted other arguments to justify the constitutionality of protective duties. He maintained that power over foreign commerce had been generally understood at the time the Constitution was adopted to embrace a protective authority, that it had been so applied for many years by Great Britain, "whose commercial vocabulary is the parent of ours." He alleged that as a result of this understanding of the subject, the States, many of which had already provided encouragement for manufactures, clearly intended that Congress should have authority to impose protective tariffs when they relinquished control over foreign commerce.[2] He cited the fact that in the First Congress not a doubt was raised as to the constitutionality of protectionism although a number of protective measures were actually introduced: several by members from Virginia in favor of coal, hemp, and beef, and one by a member from South Carolina in favor of hemp.[3] None of them had revenue for its primary object, and one of them would have excluded revenue altogether since it prohibited imports of the commodity

[1] Letter to Professor Davis, 1832, *Writings* (Cong. ed.), vol. IV, p. 250.

[2] Letter to Joseph C. Cabell, March 22, 1827, *Writings* (Hunt ed.), vol. IX, pp. 284-86.

[3] *Cf. Annals of Congress*, vol. I, pp. 149-51.

named. Besides, the preamble to the tariff bill as a whole contained the express avowal that protection was an object. If any doubt on the point of constitutionality had existed, these declarations could not have failed to evoke it, Madison argued.[1] He seemed to attach considerable importance also to the fact that the constitutionality of protectionism "had been agreed to, or at least acquiesced in," by all branches of the government, by the States, and by the people at large, "with a few exceptions," for a period of forty years.[2]

Like most so-called strict constructionists in our history Madison had difficulty in following a path of consistency. In one or two instances, notably in relation to foreign commerce, he conceded to the national government powers which were not definitely granted or even necessarily implied by the Constitution. The reasons for such an attitude are perhaps not far to seek. He was enough of a nationalist to believe that the government should be vested with sufficient energy and authority to protect the country's interests against foreign states and to assume control over any function vitally necessary to the country's welfare which the Constitution had not made other provision for or prohibited altogether. As President during a period of war he apparently found the need for a United States Bank urgent enough to overcome his earlier constitutional scruples on that issue. Probably most important of all was the effect of his position as leader of a political party—a party that gloried in the acquisition of Louisiana, conspired for the conquest of East and West Florida, and

[1] Letter to Professor Davis, 1832, *Writings* (Cong. ed.), vol. IV, p. 247.

[2] *Ibid.*, vol. IV, p. 246.

clamored for internal improvements and high protective tariffs as vociferously as any group of Federalists. Nevertheless, Madison was sincerely devoted to the principles of a federal system, which he regarded as the greatest contribution ever made by any people to the science of government; and in spite of his rather generous enlargements of the national authority, he never went as far in that direction as did Marshall, Story, and Webster.

### VIEWS OF NULLIFICATION AND SECESSION

Of all the political issues that agitated the public mind in the first half of the nineteenth century the two most important from the theoretical standpoint were nullification and secession. Madison's views regarding these issues derived logically and unavoidably from his theories of the Union and the Constitution. As we have already seen, he regarded the Union as a union of States formed by the people in the States as sovereign political communities not by the State governments. The Constitution was to him a compact among the States in the sense of political societies, and it was the instrument by which the people, that is a majority of them in each State, surrendered a portion of their sovereignty to the government of the Union. The only parties to the compact, however, were the States as political societies, not the people as individuals nor the governments of the States.

According to Madison it is precisely because the Constitution is a compact that it is binding upon all of the States. A State has no more right than an individual to violate solemn engagements.[1] "Compact is the basis and essence

[1] Letter to W. C. Rives, March 12, 1833, *Writings* (Hunt ed.), vol. IX, p. 513.

of free government," he maintained, "and no right to disregard it belongs to a party till released by causes of which the other parties have an equal right to judge."[1] Each of the parties has an equal right to decide whether the compact has been violated. If one insists that it has, the others have an equal right to contend that it is still valid and to demand its execution.[2] No one party can throw off its obligations at will or be liberated from them without the consent of the others. In case of such a unilateral attempt to break the compact, the other parties have the right to take such measures as may be necessary to prevent its dissolution.[3]

So far Madison's theory of the relation of the States to the Union would not appear to differ much from the views of Webster, Jackson, and other nationalists who regarded the Constitution as a kind of executed contract which no one party could abrogate without the consent of the others.[4] How then does Madison come to be identified in the popular mind with the States' rights movement? The answer is to be found in the fact that he was the author of the Virginia Resolutions of 1798, in which he is commonly supposed to have advocated nullification and perhaps even secession. It now becomes necessary, there-

[1] Letter to N. P. Trist, Jan. 18, 1833, *Writings* (Cong. ed.), vol. IV, p. 268.

[2] Letter to C. E. Haynes, Aug. 27, 1832, *Writings* (Hunt ed.), vol. IX, p. 483.

[3] Letter to N. P. Trist, Feb. 15, 1830, *Writings* (Hunt ed.), vol. IX, pp. 355-56 note.

[4] Daniel Webster, *Works*, 15th ed., Boston, 1869, vol. III, pp. 467-68; Andrew Jackson, Message to South Carolina, Richardson, *op. cit.*, vol. II, p. 649.

fore, to examine the doctrines of these Resolutions and Madison's own interpretations of them.

The Virginia Resolutions declared the Union to be a "Union of States" and affirmed that the powers of the Federal government resulted from "the compact to which the States are parties." These powers were avowed to be enumerated powers, "limited by the plain sense and intention of the instrument constituting that compact." The author then declared that in case of a "deliberate, palpable, and dangerous exercise of other powers not granted by the said compact, the States, who are parties thereto, have the right and are in duty bound to interpose for arresting the progress of the evil, and for maintaining within their respective limits the authorities, rights, and liberties appertaining to them." The Resolutions referred apprehensively to a tendency recently manifested by the Federal government to enlarge its powers by forced constructions of the Constitution, and to a design to interpret general phrases of that instrument in such a way that the purpose and meaning of the enumerations would be destroyed and the States consolidated into one sovereignty. The inevitable result, it was claimed, would be the transformation of the republic into an "absolute, or at least, a mixed monarchy." Finally, the author condemned the Alien and Sedition Acts as unconstitutional and called upon the other States to co-operate with Virginia "in maintaining unimpaired the authorities, rights, and liberties reserved to the States respectively, or to the people."[1]

The claim has actually been made that these Resolutions implied the right of resisting the Federal government by force, and that the Virginia legislature, with the sanction of

[1] *Writings* (Hunt ed.), vol. VI, pp. 326-31.

Madison and Jefferson, launched a program of military preparations with that object in view. Albert J. Beveridge, for example, asserts: "The Republican spirit was running high. The Virginia legislature provided for an armory in Richmond to resist the 'encroachments' of the national government."[1] A recent author has shown, however, that there is no foundation for such a claim. He explains that the military preparations referred to did not mark the adoption of a new policy. "They were part of a consistent policy undertaken before the Alien and Sedition Acts were passed, even before they could reasonably have been expected, and had nothing to do with opposition to them." He maintains the real cause that had led Virginia to give more attention to her military establishment was the danger of foreign war which was then threatening the whole country. No purpose of combating the Federal government was involved at all.[2]

In 1799 Madison, at the instigation of the Virginia House of Delegates, of which he was at the time a member, drafted a sixty page Report on the Virginia Resolutions. Neither in this document nor in any of the letters which he wrote against the South Carolina nullificationists in 1832 and the years following can any evidence be found that he ever advocated armed resistance against the Federal government or disruption of the Union. When he recommended "interposition" by a State to arrest the progress of Federal encroachments, he seems to have meant very little more than an invitation to other States to condemn the evil, and to

[1] *Life of John Marshall*, New York, 1919, vol. II, p. 406.

[2] Philip G. Davidson, "Virginia and the Alien and Sedition Laws," *American Historical Review*, vol. XXXVI (1931), pp. 336-42.

plan measures of co-operation that would compel the general government to repeal its obnoxious acts. These measures might consist of remonstrances, of the initiation of impeachments and amendments to the Constitution, or of concerted action among the States to obtain a change of the representation in Congress.[1] He thought that most ordinary cases could be settled by an appeal to the Federal judiciary, unless that department had also been a party to the usurpations.[2] But whatever the measures adopted, they would have to be concurrent and not an expression of the will of an individual State.

In his later writings Madison condemned the South Carolina theory of nullification and denied that it had ever been contemplated by the Virginia Resolutions. He repudiated the doctrine that any State could by solitary action declare a law of Congress unconstitutional, arrest the operation of that law within its own territory, and at the same time maintain its adherence to the Constitution. Such a doctrine would reduce the Constitution to a mere treaty and make the States as independent and sovereign in their relations with one another as they were under the Articles of Confederation. It would proclaim the Federal government to be no government at all, but a mere agency, a kind of power of attorney, revocable at the will of any of the parties granting it.[3] It would assert the vicious principle that any one of the parties to a compact has the right to take

[1] Outline on the Constitution, *Writings* (Hunt ed.), vol. IX, p. 353; see also *Federalist* (Lodge ed.), No. 44, p. 283, and No. 46, p. 296, in which are definitely foreshadowed the doctrines of the Virginia Resolutions.

[2] Letter to Joseph C. Cabell, Sept. 7, 1829, *Writings* (Hunt ed.), vol. IX, pp. 347-51.

[3] Notes on Nullification, *Writings* (Hunt ed.), vol. IX, p. 598.

for granted that its construction is the infallible one, and to act upon it against the intepretation of all the other parties having an equal right to construe the compact.[1]

Madison maintained in opposition to this theory his famous doctrine of divided sovereignty. He affirmed that no State retains under the Constitution absolute sovereign power. When the Union was established, the States collectively, acting through the majority in each, surrendered a portion of their sovereignty to the general government. They made the latter a true government and not a mere agent to execute the will of the States. Since all of the States are parties to the constitutional compact, no one of them can construe that compact in disregard of the rights and wishes of the others. The authority of the States collectively which created the Constitution is supreme over the general government and over any individual State. This authority alone can "interpose" for the preservation of the original division of sovereignty under the political compact. But even this interposition must be confined, in all ordinary cases at least, to constitutional methods.[2]

If an individual State has no constitutional right to nullify a law of Congress, no more does it have a constitutional right by unilateral action to secede from and disrupt the

[1] *Ibid.*, vol. IX, p. 599.

[2] *Ibid.*, vol. IX, pp. 576-81. Madison was guilty of at least a minor inconsistency in his defense of the ultimate right of the States collectively to interpret the division of sovereignty. The Virginia Resolutions were adopted by the State legislature, and they had invited similar action by the legislatures of other States. The people in the States, however, not the State governments, were the parties to the constitutional compact, according to his own contention. He admitted this inconsistency in a letter to Jefferson in December, 1798. *Writings* (Hunt ed.), vol. VI, p. 328 note.

Union. Madison avowed that since the Union is based on a compact among the people incorporated as States, no State can at pleasure withdraw therefrom and set up for itself. The very nature of a compact implies that all of the parties are bound by equal obligations under it. No one party can repudiate these obligations or be liberated from them without the consent of the others. The compact can only be dissolved by the consent of all the parties to it, or at least by a majority of them. An attempt by one of them at its own pleasure to annul it would give to the others the option of acquiescing in the annulment or of attempting to prevent it. All of the States in the Union have a vital interest in preserving the Constitution and the political system established by it; they are under no obligation to suffer a wanton violation of that interest at the whim of one of their number. The Union according to Madison's theory is not a mere alliance or confederacy from which any member can withdraw whenever it may be to its own advantage to do so; on the contrary, it is a political society, a state, created by a solemn agreement among its members, who endowed it with sovereign powers in order that their peace and happiness might be enhanced.[1] Madison quite evidently believed that the States stood in somewhat the same relation to the Union as did the individual citizens to the particular States of which they were inhabitants. No more in the former case than in the latter could the solitary member have any constitutional right to dissolve the political society.

Madison made one important exception to his general denial of the right of secession. He admitted that a State

[1] Letter to N. P. Trist, Feb. 15, 1830, *Writings* (Hunt ed.), vol. IX, p. 356 note.

suffering intolerable oppression from the Federal government or from the other members of the Union would have the right to shake off the yoke, to withdraw from the compact in the same way that an individual would have the right to go into exile or to expatriate himself if oppressed beyond endurance by the State of which he was a citizen. But this right, he maintained, is a *natural* right, not a *constitutional* right. It is one of the essential rights included in the law of nature akin to the right of revolution. It is never surrendered when a political society is formed; indeed it cannot be, for like all natural rights it is inalienable. It is the *ultima ratio* under all governments whatever their form.[1] Persons inclined to be hypercritical might consider this admission of a *natural* right of secession in extreme cases a fundamental weakness in Madison's theory since determination of the extent of "intolerable oppression" would necessarily rest in the last resort with the State itself. Nevertheless, the admission was essential for one who conceived of the foundation of political society in terms of the *Naturrecht* philosophy. The political compact is formed, according to this philosophy, in order that the individual members of society may have greater security in the enjoyment of those natural rights which are essential to their happiness, not in order to destroy those rights. The parties to the compact must therefore retain the ultimate right, by individual action, to protect themselves from unbearable oppression by withdrawing from the compact. Otherwise they would occupy a meaner condition under political society than they did in the state of nature, and

[1] Outline on the Constitution, *Writings* (Hunt ed.), vol. IX, p. 353; letter to Robert Y. Hayne, April, 1830, *Writings* (Hunt ed.), vol. IX, p. 387 note.

the formation of the compact would have been a curse rather than an advantage.

It has been intimated several times already that Lockian concepts greatly influenced if they did not dominate Madison's political thinking. This was particularly true in regard to his theories of nullification and secession. He conceived of the Union as a political society formed by a compact among the States as sovereign communities. The surrender of sovereignty which they made to the government of the Union was analogous to the surrender by individuals, when a political society is formed, of the right to enforce the law of nature. Locke maintained that in the event of a controversy between the government and some of the people, the proper umpire should be the body of the people, and that the people should be the judge whether the prince or the legislative had acted contrary to its trust.[1] In the same way Madison argued that controversies between the general government and some of the States should be decided by the body of the States, and that the States collectively should judge of encroachments or usurpations by the Federal authority. It was on the basis also of Lockian principles that Madison developed his doctrine of the *natural* right of secession. In the state of nature, according to Locke, every individual has an inalienable right of self-preservation which must include the right of shaking off the burdens of political society when they become too grievous to be borne.[2] The individual State in Madison's view had the same right, but of course to be exercised only under conditions absolutely intolerable.

[1] *Second Treatise on Civil Government* (Everyman ed.), pp. 241-42.

[2] *Ibid.*, pp. 184-85.

The belief that Madison's theory furnished a basis for the doctrines of the South Carolina nullificationists would seem to have very little foundation in fact. Both their premises and their conclusions were essentially different. Madison contended that sovereignty had been divided between the States and the general government; the South Carolina school argued that sovereignty by its very nature could not be divided, that it had been retained entirely by the States. Madison believed in a state of nature, in natural rights reserved when the political compact was entered into, and in government established by agreement; Calhoun and his colleagues dismissed the state of nature as a mere fiction, and maintained that life under government is the natural and necessary condition of man. Madison regarded the Constitution as an executed contract, which had bound the parties thereto under permanent obligations subject only to collective interpretation; the nullificationists viewed the Constitution as a continuing contract, adhered to by each State for its own convenience, and subject to construction by the individual State. Finally, Madison refused to admit anything more than a *natural* right of secession to be exercised only as a means of self-preservation; the South Carolina philosophers defended an absolute *legal* right of any State as an individual sovereign to arrest the operation of a Federal law within its borders or to withdraw from the Union.[1] A wider cleavage in fundamental principles could scarcely be imagined.

[1] For the doctrines of the South Carolina nullificationists see Charles E. Merriam, *American Political Theories*, pp. 267-84.

SIX

# Theory of Legislative, Executive and Judicial Powers

THAT a free government should be organized on the basis of three separate departments was a leading axiom of Madison's philosophy. He believed that only by this means could the liberties of the people be assured of protection. Under the influence of this conviction he looked with suspicion upon any proposal to strengthen one department at the expense of another, or to give one department control over another. In the Philadelphia Convention he opposed that part of the Virginia Plan which provided for the election of the executive by the legislature. He was afraid that this would make the executive branch dependent upon the legislative, particularly inasmuch as it was proposed to make the executive eligible for re-election.[1] For the same reason he condemned a proposal to give the Senate power to try the President in case of impeachment. He thought that such cases should be tried by some kind of special tribunal representing both the legislative and judicial branches.[2]

Throughout his public career Madison labored to preserve the separation of powers as a basic principle of the American Constitution. He did not insist that there should be no mixture of powers whatever among the three depart-

[1] Farrand, *Records of the Federal Convention*, vol. II, pp. 34, 56.
[2] *Ibid.*, vol. II, p. 551.

ments; he recognized that a degree of fusion, of legislative and executive powers especially, was essential to make the principle serve its intended purpose. He did insist, however, that no one department should gain a preponderance over the others, and he consistently strove to maintain what he regarded as the original balance of powers under the Constitution. To preserve this balance he found it necessary at times to support the claims of different departments as one or another of them appeared to be in danger of losing its proper prerogative. This was not his sole motive in every instance, for he was naturally influenced at times in favor of a particular branch by the circumstances of practical politics or by his political and economic theories.

### THEORY OF LEGISLATIVE POWER

During the colonial period and the period of the Confederation there was a definite tendency in America to establish a governmental system of legislative supremacy. Several factors worked to produce this result. In the seventeenth century Sir Edward Coke's fusion of legislative and judicial powers in the "High Court of Parliament" doubtless had some influence. In the eighteenth century the Blackstonian theory of legislative omnipotence gained a rather wide acceptance in this country. Moreover, as a result of the scarcity of lawyers and judges and the lack of a recognized code of law, colonial legislatures were compelled to assume a great many judicial and administrative functions. Then came the Revolution and with it the collapse of the royal judicial system and the growth of a strong desire to deal in summary fashion with the enemies of the new order. As a consequence there was scarcely a judicial function that was not swept into the legislative orbit.[1]

The end of the Revolution brought a reaction against this tendency. The State law-making bodies under the propulsion of "levelling influences" began to interfere with the normal processes in the courts, suspending judicial actions, modifying or annulling judgments, and even determining the merits of disputes. These impairments of "the steady dispensation of justice," as Madison phrased it, together with rag money laws exerted a compelling influence toward the erection of limitations on legislative power. The natural rights philosophy of John Locke, which had been popularized during the Revolution, and the teachings of Montesquieu also had their effect. The result was a denial of legislative omnipotence and the incorporation of safeguards against it in the new Constitution.[2]

One of the most vigorous opponents of the doctrine of legislative supremacy during the period of the adoption of the Constitution was James Madison. He regarded as unmitigated evils all of the fruits that the doctrine had recently borne in the States. The inflationary schemes of the local legislatures and the interferences with the administration of justice had been profoundly disturbing to his love of stability and his devotion to property as a sacred right. With these impressions fresh in his mind he declared in Number 48 of the *Federalist* that the sovereign source of danger in a republic is legislative aggrandizement. He

[1] E. S. Corwin, "The Progress of Constitutional Theory between the Declaration of Independence and the Meeting of the Philadelphia Convention," *American Historical Review*, vol. XXX (1925), p. 515.

[2] *Ibid.*, pp. 514-20.

demonstrated that there are several reasons why the legislative department inclines to extend the sphere of its activity and to draw all power into its "impetuous vortex." In the first place it is sufficiently numerous to feel all the passions which propel a multitude to action. Furthermore its constitutional powers are more extensive and less capable of precise definition than those of any other branch. He contended, however, that it is especially its power to levy and expend revenues that gives a legislature the capacity to usurp the functions of the other divisions of the government: it controls their very life blood.[1] He seemed at this time to underestimate the influence which an aggressive personality in the executive office could exert in overcoming the legal advantages of an ambitious legislature.

As the administration of President Washington revealed an increasing disposition to dominate the government, Madison shifted his line of attack. He was inclined from this time on to exalt the legislative branch as a check against executive despotism. He challenged the exclusive control of the executive over the treaty-making function and over the conduct of foreign relations. Neither did his attitude change when he became President. Like the other members of the Virginia Dynasty he appeared to think of the executive as primarily the agent of the people's representatives in Congress. He did not make use of any of the usual methods employed by Presidents to impose his will upon the legislators. He made few recommendations for legislative action, and he resorted to the veto power only six times.[2] It was largely due to his influence that by

[1] Lodge edition, pp. 309-10.

[2] Henry Jones Ford, *op. cit.*, p. 165; Richardson, *op. cit.*, vol. I, pp. 465-586.

the end of Monroe's second term the government of the United States had been quite definitely transformed into a government of Congressional supremacy, a supremacy which was not overthrown until 1828-1829 when the Jacksonian Revolution exalted the President into the supreme representative of the majority will and reduced the members of Congress to mere brokers for the districts that elected them.[1]

Attention must now be given to a more particular analysis of Madison's conception of the powers of Congress; and the point must first of all be emphasized that by the powers of Congress he meant primarily the powers of the House of Representatives. He seemed generally to regard the Senate as a kind of executive council which would exercise a veto power over legislation and approve or disapprove the President's action in making treaties and appointments to office. In actual fact during the first forty years of our national history the House virtually was the legislative branch of the government. It usually originated important measures, and most of the great debates on vital public questions took place within its halls.[2]

First among the powers which Madison thought Congress should possess may be mentioned the power to interpret the Constitution. He did not regard this as the exclusive prerogative of the judiciary, although he admitted that in the ordinary course of things it would appertain to that branch. He insisted, nevertheless, that it was not the intention of the authors of the fundamental law to give the judges a monopoly of that power, particularly in cases in-

[1] Henry Jones Ford, *op. cit.*, pp. 246, 262.

[2] *Ibid.*, p. 165.

volving disagreements among the three departments regarding the scope of their authority. Each department, he argued, should be the proper judge of its own objects, and should have the supreme right to mark out the limits of its own power. Neither the executive nor the judiciary should have any right to question an interpretation by Congress of what constitutes legislative authority. Only in this way, he maintained, could the principle of the separation of powers be preserved.[1]

But his conception of the power of Congress to engage in exposition of the Constitution did not end here. He insisted that the national legislature had at least a limited power to decide questions of constitutionality that had been left in doubt by the written organic law. To be sure no one Congress would have the right to settle the issue; but over a considerable time the deliberate and reiterated assertions of a particular constitutional construction, by a succession of Congresses, should be taken to possess a *de facto* validity and should therefore be entitled to the respect of all branches of the government.[2] In other words, he believed in a kind of rule of *stare decisis* for legislative as well as judicial interpretation of the Constitution. He appeared to think a course of such legislative expositions, sufficiently deliberate, uniform, and definite, would really be an expression of the sovereign public will almost tantamount to a constitutional amendment.[3] It was partly on this basis that he considered the question of the constitutionality of

[1] *Annals of Congress,* vol. I, p. 501; vol. V, p. 773.

[2] Letter to C. J. Ingersoll, June 25, 1831, *Writings* (Cong. ed.), vol. IV, pp. 185-86.

[3] Letter to C. E. Haynes, Feb. 25, 1831, *Writings* (Hunt ed.), vol. IX, p. 443.

the United States Bank finally to have been settled,[1] and he regarded legislative construction of the Constitution as an important factor in favor of the legality of protective tariffs.[2] After he had retired from public life, he even suggested that it might be used to sanction Federal expenditures for internal improvements.[3] He maintained, however, that a careful distinction should be drawn between cases where Congress opposes the will of its constituents, as happened in the enactment of the Alien and Sedition Laws, and cases where the legislative will is in harmony with the will of a majority of the people and the States. Only in cases of the latter sort would Congressional exposition of the Constitution have any validity.[4]

With his fear of the development of executive tyranny through an abuse of the war powers, it was natural that Madison should have insisted upon the right of Congress to exercise some degree of control over the conduct of foreign relations. In particular he denounced the conduct of foreign affairs by the President in such a way as practically to force Congress into a declaration of war. He denied the right of the executive to make any commitment implying an obligation to go to war. He maintained that such a commitment would not be binding upon Congress against its own judgment. Unconstitutional devices of this kind, he insisted, would cheat the people out of "the best

[1] *Ibid.*, vol. IX, p. 443.

[2] Letter to Professor Davis, 1832, *Writings* (Cong. ed.), vol. IV, p. 246.

[3] Letter to Jefferson, Feb. 17, 1825, *Writings* (Cong. ed.), vol. III, p. 483.

[4] Letter to N. P. Trist, Feb. 7, 1827, *Writings* (Cong. ed.), vol. III, p. 551.

ingredients in their government, the safeguards of peace which is the greatest of their blessings."[1]

The question of Congressional control over the conduct of foreign affairs was directly involved in Franco-American relations in the decade of the 1790's. In 1778, while the American States were engaged in the Revolution, the government of Louis XVI had negotiated a treaty of alliance with the Continental Congress. Fifteen years later France became embroiled in a war with Great Britain. The treaty of 1778 had never been formally abrogated, and the question now arose whether the United States was bound to go to the aid of France. Mainly upon the advice of Hamilton, President Washington decided to issue a proclamation of neutrality. Madison made this the occasion of a vigorous criticism of executive encroachment upon the prerogative of the legislature. He denied the authority of the President to determine the disposition of the United States in regard to war or peace by issuing a proclamation of neutrality. The right to decide the question whether the duty and interest of the nation require neutrality or participation in war, he maintained, belongs to Congress. Since the legislature has the exclusive power under the Constitution to declare war, the logical presumption must be that the power to determine *whether* war shall be declared also vests exclusively in the legislature.[2] Consequently Congress alone can have authority to decide whether a *causus foederis* has arisen under a treaty of alliance.[3]

[1] Letter to Jefferson, April 2, 1798, *Writings* (Hunt ed.), vol. VI, pp. 313-14.

[2] Letter to Jefferson, June 13, 1793, *Writings* (Hunt ed.), vol. VI, p. 131.

[3] Letters of Helvidius, No. II, *Writings* (Hunt ed.), vol. VI, p. 160.

Finally, according to Madison, Congress has a very definite control over the treaty-making function. The treaty power is a limited power, and the President and the Senate cannot extend it to any objects that their arbitrary notions may consider appropriate. Where a treaty contemplates effects of a distinctly legislative character or purports to repeal an existing law, it cannot become valid without the approval of the House of Representatives.[1] The treaty-making power cannot be superior to the law-making power. It is inconsistent with the Constitution that laws should be repealed by treaties; laws can be repealed only by laws. That the American people, so jealous of the purse and the sword, should have intended to put both into the hands of the President and the Senate and make Congress the mere herald to proclaim war, the agent to recruit armies, and the cashier to pay out money for their maintenance and equipment is utterly beyond belief.[2]

Madison argued further that omnipotence of the President and Senate in regard to treaties would be entirely incompatible with a political system marked throughout by limitations and checks. If the treaty power were unrestricted, then all the constitutional limitations on the power of Congress would be meaningless. The President and the Senate could levy taxes on exports, make appropriations for longer than two years, or grant a preference to the ports of one State over those of another. Neither would the powers granted exclusively to Congress mean anything, for the President and the Senate by means of a treaty could plunge the country into war, raise armies, regulate foreign commerce, or borrow money. Save in connection with a few

[1] *Annals of Congress*, vol. V, pp. 777-78.

[2] *Writings* (Hunt ed.), vol. VI, pp. 295-300.

minor objects, the functions of Congress would be rendered largely superfluous.[1]

Madison contended that the constitutional provision making treaties a part of the supreme law of the land means a supremacy in respect of State constitutions and laws and not in relation to laws of the United States. He insisted that in all cases where the Federal Constitution has given specific powers to Congress every exercise of the treaty power requires the sanction and co-operation of the House of Representatives. He admitted that the legislature would have to use discretion, allowing proper weight to the reasons which had led to the treaty, but he maintained that there should be an actual exercise of reason, of deliberation, an expression of legislative will, not a mere perfunctory enactment of laws to give effect to the treaty. The objection that no treaty could be made at all if the concurrence of the House were required he held to be invalid. The President and the Senate would be just as likely to make a bad treaty as the House would be to throw objections in the path of a good one after it was made.[2]

As a matter of fact Madison really took the position that treaties are a species of laws and that the power to make them is more of a legislative than an executive function. He arrived at this conclusion on the basis of reasoning substantially as follows: The treaty-making power is vested jointly in the President and the Senate, and although this circumstance alone would not necessarily exclude the power from the executive class since the Senate also shares in making appointments, there are other considerations which

[1] *Annals of Congress*, vol. V, pp. 490-91.

[2] *Ibid.*, vol. V, pp. 487-94.

indicate that the making of treaties is regarded by the Constitution as different from a mere executive function and as properly belonging under the legislative description. For example, a two-thirds vote in the Senate is necessary for the approval of a treaty, whereas in the case of appointments a majority vote suffices. The two-thirds requirement appears to have been intended by the fathers of the Constitution as a compensation for lack of participation by the House of Representatives, which for practical reasons had to be excluded. Furthermore, treaties frequently partake not only of an external character, but of an internal or municipal character as well. That is, their operation extends in some cases to objects of a domestic nature, in exactly the same manner as ordinary laws. Finally, the Constitution itself affirms the legislative character of treaties. They are declared to have the force and operation of laws, and the courts are to be governed by them in the same manner as by ordinary statutes.[1]

### THEORY OF EXECUTIVE POWER

Perhaps it has been made evident already that Madison's conception of executive power was quite different from that which prevails at the present time. Despotism of one sort or another always seemed to him an ever-present danger; and after the new government had been set up, he appeared to think that executive despotism was most of all to be feared. Abhorrence of executive tyranny inspired a great many of his political attitudes. For example, his opposition to absorption of State sovereignty by the

[1] Letters of Helvidius, No. 1, *Writings* (Hunt ed.), vol. VI, pp. 147-48.

national government was prompted in large part by his fear that a consolidated government would lead to monarchy. Concentration of all powers in the national authority, he maintained, would increase the legislative burden of Congress to an intolerable degree, and would result in the surrender of more and more of the legislative prerogative to the executive. In addition, the number of offices, honors, and emoluments at the disposal of the President would be greatly increased. The combined effect of the extraordinary expansion of executive power and patronage would enable the chief magistrate by quiet means to insure his re-election time after time, and ultimately to regulate the succession in whatever way he pleased; or, by giving so vast an importance to the office, would render Presidential elections so violent and corrupt that the public in disgust might demand an hereditary succession.[1]

At no time in his life did Madison advocate a government of Presidential supremacy. Even during the period when he was most critical of the tyranny of legislative majorities, he never proposed executive domination as a remedy. On the contrary, he appeared always to assume that the powers of the executive should be rather strictly limited. In a pamphlet which he wrote in 1795 he avowed that it was essential to republican government that "the assumption and extension of discretionary powers" in the executive department should not be tolerated, and he vigorously denied the right of the President to exercise during a recess of Congress any powers normally belonging to the legislature, such as declaring the existence of a state of

[1] Report on the Virginia Resolutions, *Writings* (Hunt ed.), vol. VI, pp. 358-59.

war, raising armies, or creating offices.[1] During his own administration as President he took the position that he had no discretion in enforcing either judicial decisions or acts of Congress.[2]

In two instances, it is true, Madison did recommend an enlargement of Presidential powers and privileges, but only for the purpose of preventing greater evils and preserving the separation of powers. In the first of these cases he recommended that the executive should be made eligible to succeed himself. He feared that otherwise the incumbent in office might be encouraged to resort to desperate enterprises to attain what would not be attainable by legitimate means. Moreover, he was afraid that in a crisis a prohibition against re-election might have the effect of excluding a choice which would be necessary to the public safety.[3]

In the second instance Madison urged that the President should be almost entirely exempted from legislative control in making appointments to and removals from public office. He denied that the Senate had any right to interfere with a nomination made by the President, more than to accept it or to reject it; it could not change the conditions on which the appointment would take effect, for example.[4] During his own administration he refused to consult with a committee of the Senate that had been chosen to confer with him regarding the appointment of a min-

[1] *Political Observations*, Manuscript, Columbia University Library, New York.

[2] *American State Papers, Miscellaneous*, vol. II, p. 12.

[3] Observations on Draught of a Constitution for Virginia, *Writings* (Hunt ed.), vol. V, pp. 289-90.

[4] Letter to Monroe, Sept. 24, 1822, *Writings* (Hunt ed.), vol. IX, pp. 112-13.

ister to Sweden.[1] He also denied the power of Congress to limit the tenure of officers appointed by the President, contending that this would be an encroachment on the constitutional attributes of the executive. He maintained that the tenure of office of Presidential appointees, the judges and quasi-judicial officers excepted, should depend on the pleasure of the President alone. If a law could displace an officer at the end of every four years, he argued, it could do so at the end of every year, and control over the executive branch would pass very largely into the hands of the legislature. The degree of independence necessary to make the former department an effective check upon the latter would be practically destroyed.[2]

Madison considered it even more essential that the President should be free from Senatorial interference with removals from office. He adduced the following reasons in support of this view: If there is any principle in the Constitution more sacred than another, it is the principle of the separation of powers. The Constitution provides that the legislative power shall be vested in Congress, the executive power in a President of the United States, and the judicial power in a Supreme Court and other courts. It was clearly intended that all powers coming under these respective heads should be exercised by the department indicated, save where exceptions were expressly made. Now the appointing and removal powers are executive powers, and, without qualification in the Constitution, they would both unquestionably belong to the President. The appointing

[1] Special Message to the Senate; reprinted in *Writings* (Hunt ed.), vol. VIII, pp. 250-51.

[2] Letter to Monroe, Dec. 28, 1820, *Writings* (Hunt ed.), vol. IX, pp. 43-44.

power is qualified by giving the Senate a share in it; but that is an exception, and Congress has no authority to prescribe any further exceptions.[1]

In addition, the Constitution imposes upon the President the duty of taking care that the laws be faithfully executed. It must therefore have been intended that he should possess every species of power which is a necessary means to that end. An essential means of executing the laws is the power to supervise and control the official conduct of subordinates, and the removal power is a necessary incident to such control. To give the Senate a share in the removal power would be to enable that body to force the President to continue in office his most important subordinates, including Cabinet members, no matter how hostile and obstructionist they might be.[2] Besides, it is a basic principle of our constitutional system that there should be the highest possible degree of responsibility in the executive officers, and it is only by vesting the removal power in the President alone that this can be attained. The President will thus be made responsible for the behavior of every one of his subordinates, and he will be subject to impeachment if he keeps unworthy men in office.[3]

Last of all, there are risks in giving the Senate control over the removal power. It is in reality a permanent body. It is responsible to State legislatures instead of the people. It embodies the aristocratic quality in the government. The dangers of confiding this power to the President alone are insignificant by comparison. The exercise of his authority

[1] *Annals of Congress*, vol. I, p. 463.

[2] Letter to John M. Patton, March 24, 1834, *Writings* (Hunt ed.), vol. IX, p. 535.

[3] *Annals of Congress*, vol. I, p. 497.

is surrounded by numerous restraints. He is impeachable before the Senate for any malfeasance in office. Finally, his official record is subject to approval or condemnation by the community at large at the end of every four years, and he will inevitably be displaced if his administration stands in disrepute.[1]

It should be added that Madison had no sympathy with the idea that the appointing and removal powers should be used by the President for the purpose of building up a political machine or for the advancement of his own policies. He denounced severely the doctrine that public offices are the spoils of victory, the personal property of the successful candidate for the Presidency to be given as prizes for party services, or to be used to reward those who support and punish those who do not support the dispenser of them.[2]

In all cases other than the appointing and removal powers Madison argued for a limitation rather than an expansion of the Presidential prerogative. He denied, for instance, the right of the chief magistrate, on his own responsibility, to recognize or refuse to recognize foreign governments. He admitted that there might be cases in which respect for the principles of liberty and the other rights of humanity would require that a government, whether new or old, should be treated as an illegitimate despotism. He maintained, however, that these would be rare and momentous issues by no means to be decided by so limited an organ of the general will as the executive of the United States. He admitted also that the Constitution

[1] *Ibid.*, vol. I, pp. 497-99.

[2] Letter to Edward Coles, Aug. 29, 1834, *Writings* (Hunt ed.), vol. IX, p. 539.

gives the President authority to receive ambassadors, other public ministers, and consuls; but he denied that it was ever intended that this should be magnified into the important power of recognizing or refusing to recognize governments of foreign states. In agreement with the view of Hamilton as expressed in Number 69 of the *Federalist*, he contended that receiving the diplomatic agents of other countries would be "more a matter of dignity than of authority," and would not imply a right to pass upon the validity of revolutions.[1]

According to Madison the President has no discretion whatever respecting a change in the government of a foreign country. He cannot even refuse to receive public ministers on that account. If he declines to receive an ambassador, it must be on some other ground. The question of the *right* of a government to rule over a nation is for that nation alone to decide. "Where the fact appears to be that the government does exist, the executive must be governed by the fact, and can have no right or discretion, on account of the date or form of the government, to refuse to acknowledge it, either by rejecting its public ministers, or by any other steps taken on that account."[2]

On virtually every question pertaining to foreign relations Madison was suspicious of Presidential authority. He considered the executive the department of the government most distinguished by a propensity to war, and he avowed that it should be the practice in every state where freedom is a coveted prize to disarm the executive

[1] Letters of Helvidius, No. 3, *Writings* (Hunt ed.), vol. VI, pp. 163-64.

[2] *Ibid.*, vol. VI, p. 169.

of every means of giving effect to that propensity.[1] In the Federal Convention he recommended that the Senate should be empowered to make treaties of peace by a two-thirds vote without the concurrence of the President since the latter would derive so much prestige and power from a state of war that he might be tempted to hinder the conclusion of peace.[2] In a letter to Jefferson in 1797 he gave perhaps his most cogent reasons for this attitude of distrust of the executive. "The management of foreign affairs," he wrote, "appears to be the most susceptible of abuse of all the trusts committed to a government, because they can be concealed or disclosed, or disclosed in such parts and at such times as will best suit particular views; and because the body of the people are less capable of judging, and are more under the influence of prejudices, on that branch of their affairs, than of any other. Perhaps it is a universal truth that the loss of liberty at home is to be charged to provisions against danger, real or pretended, from abroad."[3]

From some of his declarations in the Constitutional Convention one might get the impression that Madison believed in a rather drastic use of the veto power by the executive. He most certainly did believe that a veto authority was necessary to "prevent popular or factious injustice," and to check the encroachments of the legislature.[4] Moreover, he urged the requirement of a three-fourths vote in both houses to override a veto. He feared that a two-thirds requirement would not be sufficient to prevent the

[1] *Ibid.*, vol. VI, p. 174.

[2] Farrand, *Records of the Federal Convention*, vol. II, p. 540.

[3] *Writings* (Cong. ed.), vol. I, pp. 140-41.

[4] Farrand, *Records of the Federal Convention*, vol. II, p. 587.

legislature from absorbing the powers and functions of the other departments.[1] On the other hand, he had no intention of entrusting the veto authority solely to the President. While he considered it essential that the independence of the executive should be preserved, he indicated also that his power must not be left uncontrolled, for the chief magistrate of a republic would not have great emoluments, nor "that permanent stake in the public interest" that would render him immune from the temptations of corruption. He advocated, therefore, that the right to negative laws should be vested in a council of revision composed of the President and the judges of the Supreme Court. Not only would such a council provide the necessary control over the executive, but the co-operation of the judicial talent would give to the laws a perspicuity and systematic character and inhibit the passage of unwise measures.[2]

As President, Madison appeared to regard the veto power as a mere advisory function, not as a weapon to force Congress into line with executive policy.[3] No evidence can be found that he ever threatened to veto a bill in order to compel modification of it to suit his own desires or that he ever forced Congress to enact some favored measure of his by threatening to negative a cherished project of one or both houses. In other words, he did not conceive of the President's having any *positive* control over the law-making function, and he would have regarded the use of the prestige and power of the office by some of his more recent

[1] *Ibid.*, vol. II, p. 587.
[2] *Ibid.*, vol. I, pp. 138-39.
[3] Henry Jones Ford, *op. cit.*, p. 179.

successors for the purpose of supplanting the will of the legislators as a perversion of the separation of powers.

In his Observations on the Draught of a Constitution for Virginia Madison made another very interesting suggestion in reference to the veto power. He proposed that bills before finally becoming laws should be submitted to the executive and judicial departments separately, and that if either or both should object to a bill as unconstitutional, it should be suspended from going into effect regardless of the number of members of both houses who would vote to overrule the objection. An election should then be held for members of the lower house; and if the bill were subsequently passed by a three-fourths vote in both houses, it should become a law in spite of the objections of the executive and the judiciary.[1] Here was a unique suggestion for establishing direct responsibility of government to the people, so far as questions of constitutionality were concerned. It would have operated in a way somewhat similar to the system which has recently developed in Great Britain, where in case of a conflict between the Cabinet and Parliament, the people, by means of an election to the House of Commons, decide the issue.

## THEORY OF JUDICIAL POWER

The subject of judicial power in American political theory is a difficult and complicated one, involving as it does such perplexing questions as the nature of law, judicial review of legislation, and the relations of the several units and branches of the government. Madison's ideas on this subject, as well as those of his contemporaries, can be understood only in relation to a vast historical background that

[1] *Writings* (Hunt ed.), vol. V, pp. 293-94.

covered several centuries of intellectual development. A brief survey of this background is therefore necessary.

American legal theory in colonial times represented an accumulation of ideas that ran all the way back to Cicero and the Stoics and included the contributions of the medievalists, of Bracton, of Coke, and most of all, of Locke. Cicero and the Stoics furnished the idea of a law of nature, the embodiment of justice, universal, constant, and eternal. Medievalists like John of Salisbury contributed the doctrine of authority as intrinsically conditioned or limited by its very nature. Bracton and Coke evolved the conception of the common law as the primary expression of right reason, of the higher law, and therefore as a limitation upon the powers of King and Parliament. Locke was pre-eminently responsible for setting up the substantive rights of the individual as an automatic restraint upon the powers of government. But all of these limitations were in perfect accordance with a single main tradition; that is, with the tradition of a higher law of universal right, eternal reason, and abstract justice which is superior to all ordinary statutes and decrees.[1]

As a result of these different influences American lawyers and philosophers in the latter half of the eighteenth century had adopted a view of law that was quite different from the modern conception. They did not think of law in the positivist sense of the command of a superior addressed to an inferior, but mainly as the expression of eternal principles of right and reason self-evident to the minds of all enlightened men. Of course they did not regard

[1] E. S. Corwin, "The Higher Law Background of American Constitutional Law," *Harvard Law Review*, vol. XLII (1928-29), pp. 157, 172-85, 393.

statutes and decrees as examples of law in this sense; they conceived of them merely as governmental acts subject to the limitations of the higher law. They did gradually adopt the idea, however, that a written constitution was a prime example of the higher law; and while they did not take it to include the whole body of that law, they nevertheless believed that it derived its main validity from the fact of its content, from the fact that it incorporated within itself principles of intrinsic sanctity.[1]

The doctrine of judicial review was a direct outgrowth of the theory of law that has just been described. Since the belief prevailed that there were sacred principles of universal right which acted as limitations upon all authority, and since ordinary statutes were regarded as mere expressions of the will of governing agents, it was perhaps almost inevitable that some system should be developed whereby conflicts between the higher law and the inferior enactments could be settled in favor of the former. This system did not necessarily have to take the form of review of legislation by the courts; it might have conformed to the English pattern of making the legislative body the supreme judge of the validity of its own enactments. There were several reasons, however, that precluded the latter development. In the first place, the American legislatures were not judicial bodies; whereas Parliament under late medieval theory did have the status of a "high court."[2] Besides, the legislatures in this country by reason of their interferences with private rights had brought themselves

[1] A. C. McLaughlin, *The Foundations of American Constitutionalism*, pp. 107 ff.

[2] *Cf.* C. H. McIlwain, *The High Court of Parliament*, New Haven, 1910.

into disrepute with the ruling classes, and a means of curbing their power was ardently desired.

Probably the most important of all the reasons was the long series of precedents for judicial review that had been established in England and America in the seventeenth and eighteenth centuries. The first of these precedents was Coke's famous decision in Dr. Bonham's case in 1610. The renowned chief justice ruled in this case that the common law would control and adjudge "utterly void" an act of Parliament against common right or reason or impossible of performance. In America as early as 1657 a Massachusetts court in the case of Giddings *v.* Brown set aside an act of a town meeting on the ground that it conflicted with the law of nature.[1] But the most numerous and the most significant precedents on this side of the Atlantic were established in the second half of the eighteenth century. The conflict between the colonies and the mother country gave rise to frequent attacks upon the power of Parliament, and the same basis of an appeal to a higher law characterized nearly all of them. John Adams, for example, in denouncing the Stamp Act declared: "It is utterly void and of no binding force upon us; for it is against our rights as men and our privileges as Englishmen . . . Parliaments may err, they are not infallible . . . There are certain principles fixed unalterably in nature."[2]

In 1761 James Otis in the famous Writs of Assistance Case affirmed the right of an ordinary court to condemn irrevocably the enacted will of Parliament in the event

[1] Theodore F. T. Plucknett, "Bonham's Case and Judicial Review," *Harvard Law Review*, vol. XL (1926), pp. 61-62.

[2] *Quincy Reports*, 200; quoted by McLaughlin, *The Courts, the Constitution and Parties*, p. 80.

of a violation of the higher law.[1] Soon afterwards American courts began to act on that principle. A county court in Virginia in 1766 declared the Stamp Act unconstitutional and directed that it need not be obeyed.[2] And on the eve of the Declaration of Independence Judge Cushing, later a justice of the United States Supreme Court, charged a Massachusetts jury to ignore certain acts of Parliament as "void and inoperative."[3]

After independence had been secured, the courts continued the practice of the judicial veto, directed now, of course, against the legislatures of the States in their interferences with the rights of creditors and property owners. Among the examples of judicial review in this period were the Rhode Island case of Trevett *v.* Weeden, the South Carolina case of Bowman *v.* Middleton, and the North Carolina case of Bayard *v.* Singleton. In the last of these the Supreme Court of North Carolina declared invalid an act of the legislature on the definite basis of its conflict with the written constitution. It may be of significance that the attorneys who argued against the constitutionality of the statute were William R. Davie, a delegate to the Philadelphia Convention, and James Iredell, who later was appointed to the original bench of the Federal Supreme Court.[4]

What was the attitude of the fathers of the Constitution

[1] Corwin, "The Higher Law Background of American Constitutional Law," *Harvard Law Review*, vol. XLII, p. 398.

[2] McLaughlin, *The Foundations of American Constitutionalism*, p. 126.

[3] Corwin, *The Doctrine of Judicial Review*, Princeton, 1914, p. 32.

[4] *Ibid.*, p. 39.

toward judicial power? Attempts have been made to prove that they had no intention of giving to the Federal courts the power to invalidate laws of Congress and the State legislatures, but most of the available evidence supports the opposite view. The issue of judicial control was never squarely presented to the Philadelphia Convention, and some modern critics have erred completely in asserting that the framers of the Constitution rejected every proposal to establish judicial review.[1] It is true that the Convention did reject proposals to allow the judges to participate in a council of revision, and to share the veto power with the executive, but such an arrangement would be far from the equivalent of judicial review. And it is an interesting fact that some of the advocates of the council of revision scheme urged its adoption as a *supplement* to judicial review. James Wilson, for instance, avowed that the power of judges to declare laws unconstitutional was not enough. "Laws may be unjust," he argued, "may be unwise, may be dangerous, may be destructive; and yet not be so unconstitutional as to justify the judges in refusing to give them effect. Let them have a share in the revisionary power, and they will have an opportunity of taking notice of these characters of a law, and of counteracting, by the weight of their opinions, the improper views of the legislature." Madison and Gouverneur Morris supported this doctrine.[2] In view of Wilson's argument it is impossible to maintain that refusal to permit judicial collaboration in the veto

[1] See, for example, Franklin D. Roosevelt's recent contention that "Again and again the Convention voted down proposals to give justices of the Court a veto over legislation." *New York Times*, September 18, 1937, p. 4.

[2] Farrand, *Records of the Federal Convention*, vol. II, p. 22.

power was tantamount to rejection of judicial review. Indeed it would be just as logical to conclude that the Convention turned down the recommendation of Wilson, Madison, and Morris because of a belief that judicial review was quite enough, that no further authority of the judges was necessary as a check upon the legislature.

Additional evidences can also be found in the assertions of particular members of the Convention which indicate that they seem to have taken judicial review for granted as an essential part of the new government. Elbridge Gerry, for instance, referred on June 4 to the fact that "In some States the judges had already set aside laws as being against the Constitution."[1] On July 23 Madison declared that "A law violating a treaty ratified by a pre-existing law, might be respected by the judges as a law, though an unwise or perfidious one. A law violating a constitution established by the people themselves, would be considered by the judges as null and void."[2] Madison made one other assertion on the floor of the Convention which seemed to imply that the Federal courts would have the right to review acts of Congress. On August 28 he declared that "retrospective interferences" with private rights would be prohibited by the interdiction against *ex post facto* laws.[3] As the *ex post facto* clause which had been theretofore adopted by the Convention applied only to Congress and not to the States, Madison's remark appears to have been a definite recognition of the power of the judiciary to hold an act of the national legislature unconstitutional and

[1] Farrand, *Records of the Federal Convention*, vol. I, p. 97.
[2] *Ibid.*, vol. II, p. 93.
[3] *Ibid.*, vol. II, p. 440.

void.[1] It should be noted further that Gerry and Madison were not the leaders of a tiny minority on this issue. Professor Beard has shown that among the twenty-five most prominent members of the Convention, seventeen can be counted as positively in favor of a veto by the courts of unconstitutional legislation, with only three definitely on record against it.[2]

During the period when the Constitution was before the States for ratification, the idea that it provided for control of legislation by the courts was seldom even questioned.[3] Opponents of the new instrument criticized it either because they thought it would make the judiciary supreme over the representatives of the people, or because they feared that judicial enforcement of limitations upon Congress could never be an effective substitute for a bill of rights. In other words, they took for granted that judicial review had been provided for by the Convention. Hamilton replied to these criticisms in Number 78 of the *Federalist*; not by denying that judicial review was included in the Constitution, but by affirming it and insisting that it was necessary to keep the legislature within the prescribed limits of its authority and to protect individual rights.[4]

On the basis of these and other evidences many of the ablest commentators on our constitutional history have concluded that the members of the Federal Convention clearly intended that judicial review in some degree should be in-

[1] Charles Warren, *The Making of the Constitution*, Boston, 1929, p. 556 note.

[2] Charles A. Beard, *The Supreme Court and the Constitution*, New York, 1912, pp. 17-56.

[3] Corwin, *The Doctrine of Judicial Review*, p. 17.

[4] Lodge edition, p. 485.

cluded as a fundamental part of the new system of government, that it was the natural outgrowth of ideas that had been commonly accepted for many years prior to 1787, and of precedents entirely too numerous and impressive to be ignored. This is the reasoned judgment of Charles Warren and of Professors McLaughlin, Farrand, Channing, and Beard.[1] Most of the attempts to prove the opposite have sprung from a lack of knowledge of the basic principles accepted by the leading members of the Convention. Virtually all of them subscribed to the philosophy of natural rights with its doctrine of law as a product of reason and the natural order of things instead of will. They believed in a written constitution as the embodiment of a law superior to statutes, but also as a law enforceable by the courts, and binding upon all the agencies of government. Furthermore, one of the principal reasons that had brought the Philadephia Convention into existence was distrust of the recent activities of the State legislatures. "To curtail legislative power as it existed in the State constitutions in the interest, first, of an adequate national power and secondly, in the interest of private rights" made logically necessary either a Congressional veto on State laws or a judicial veto. When the former was rejected for reasons of expediency, the latter was easily accepted as a fundamental feature of the new system.[2]

Madison's theory of the power of the courts, like most

[1] McLaughlin, *The Courts, the Constitution and Parties*, p. 76; Farrand, *The Framing of the Constitution*, p. 157; Channing, *A History of the United States*, vol. III, pp. 498-502; Warren, *The Supreme Court in United States History*, Boston, 1922, vol. I, pp. 5-6; Beard, *The Supreme Court and the Constitution*, pp. 50-51.

[2] Corwin, *The Doctrine of Judicial Review*, pp. 62-63.

of the rest of his political philosophy, was a product of influences dominant at the time the Constitution was adopted; and it did not differ so very greatly from the views of his political associates of that day, although his ideas on the subject were certainly not as extreme as those of Hamilton, James Wilson, and Gouverneur Morris. But like most of his contemporaries he conceived of all governmental authority as limited by a superior law derived partly from reason and the order of nature, and partly from the ultimate sovereigns who formed the political compact. He regarded the Constitution as an expression of that law; and he considered the courts to be better qualified than any other agencies of the government to expound the Constitution, and therefore charged with the responsibility of maintaining it and protecting individuals under the general body of abstract rights.

As long as he lived Madison did not modify his earlier theories of judicial power very much. Despite significant changes in constitutional theory and practice he never abandoned his belief in the authority of the courts to pass upon the validity of legislation, especially of the sort that affected private rights. As a member of the First Congress he not only assumed the existence of such an authority, but warmly defended it. Having introduced a set of amendments to constitute a bill of rights, he declared that the courts would "consider themselves in a peculiar manner the guardians of those rights; they would be an impenetrable bulwark against every assumption of power in the Legislative or Executive; they will be naturally led to resist every encroachment upon rights stipulated for in the Constitution by the declaration of rights."[1]

[1] *Annals of Congress*, vol. I, p. 439.

When Chief Justice Marshall in the case of Marbury *v.* Madison affirmed the power of the Supreme Court to declare an act of Congress unconstitutional, Madison made no protest; neither for that matter did any of the other thirty-nine members of the Philadelphia Convention who were living at that time.[1] Madison censured the Court rather severely, however, for its decision in the case of McCulloch *v.* Maryland—on the very interesting thesis that John Marshall and his colleagues had abdicated their proper function of controlling the legislative exercise of unconstitutional powers. He believed that the opinion in this case with its broad definition of the implied powers of Congress would leave the exercise of legislative authority in the future almost unchecked. He contended that if any means are to be considered constitutional simply because they are "expedient" or "conducive to" a legitimate end, then it would have to be left to Congress to determine every means that should be employed to carry into effect a specified power. He thought that the Court could hardly presume to pass upon questions of expediency. As a consequence there would be practically no limits to legislative authority, and the whole scheme of government would be changed.[2]

At first thought, Madison may seem in these assertions to have contradicted his earlier opinions in the attack on the United States Bank. On that occasion he had declared that each department should have the right to mark out the limits of its own powers; now he appeared to be contending that the Supreme Court should determine the scope of

[1] Charles Warren, *Congress, the Constitution and the Supreme Court*, Boston, 1930, p. 127 note.

[2] Letter to Spencer Roane, Sept. 2, 1819, *Writings* (Hunt ed.), vol. VIII, pp. 449-52.

legislative power. There was no real contradiction, however. In the earlier instance he had in mind the limits of each department's powers in relation to the other departments, but now he was referring to legislative usurpations of power which he held to have been reserved by the States.

There is additional evidence that Madison regarded judicial review as an appropriate device for preserving the balance between the Federal and State authorities as well as a safeguard for individual rights. He declared on one occasion that "The Federal judiciary is the only defensive armour of the Federal government, or, rather, for the Constitution and laws of the United States. Strip it of that armour, and the door is wide open for nullification, anarchy, and convulsion."[1] In other words, the Supreme Court, through its power to veto unconstitutional laws of both the national and State legislatures, would uphold the original division of sovereignty made by the Constitution. He considered that it would be impossible to leave this function to the individual States, lest the Constitution be given a different meaning in each, and the principle of equality of the States be destroyed, since some would claim a greater measure of sovereignty than others.[2] Moreover, he appeared to believe, in the later period of his life at least, that the national government was in greater need of protection against a disturbance of the constitutional balance of power than the States. He maintained that this was particularly true inasmuch as the officers of the former were elected directly or indirectly by, and were responsible

[1] Letter to J. C. Cabell, April 1, 1833, *Writings* (Cong. ed.), vol. IV, pp. 296-97.

[2] Letter to Spencer Roane, June 29, 1821, *Writings* (Hunt ed.), vol. LX, p. 66.

to, the States; while the officers of the State governments were entirely independent, in their appointment and responsibility, of the government of the United States.[1] He assumed, however, that it would also be the function of the Court to protect the States against usurpations of power by the national government.[2]

Nevertheless, in spite of his strong conviction of the value of the Court's functions, Madison made two important qualifications of his theory of judicial control. In the first place he denied that the Supreme Court of the United States should have an absolute authority to decide controversies between the central government and the States over the respective spheres of each. He argued that there might be cases of usurpation by the Federal government of which the judiciary would never take cognizance; or that the forms of the Constitution, to which the courts are supposed to adhere, might not prove effectual safeguards against transgressions of the rights of the States. Furthermore, the Federal judiciary itself might exercise or sanction dangerous powers in excess of constitutional grants. In all such cases as these, he maintained, the people in the States, who are the parties to the compact, must have the ultimate right to judge. And this right must extend to violations by one delegated authority as much as by another, by the judicial department as well as by Congress or the President. Or as he himself expressed it in the Report on the Virginia Resolutions:

[1] Letter to Edward Everett, Aug. 28, 1830, *Writings* (Hunt ed.), vol. IX, p. 398.

[2] Letter to J. C. Cabell, Sept. 7, 1829, *Writings* (Hunt ed.), vol. IX, pp. 347-51.

> The States, then, being the parties to the constitutional compact, and in their sovereign capacity, it follows of necessity that there can be no tribunal above their authority to decide, in the last resort, whether the compact made by them be violated; and consequently, as the parties to it, they must themselves decide, in the last resort, such questions as may be of sufficient magnitude to require their interposition.[1]

In other words, the people in the States, having been the original authors of the division of sovereignty, must retain the ultimate right, in extreme cases, to adjudge disputes pertaining to that division. This did not imply, however, the right of the people in an individual State to nullify Federal laws or to secede from the Union. Only the States collectively, he maintained, could have any authority to construe the constitutional compact.

In the second place Madison qualified his theory of judicial control by denying to the courts the final power to decide questions involving controversies between departments of the government. He insisted that inasmuch as the three great branches of the government are co-ordinate and equally bound to support the Constitution, "each must in the exercise of its functions be guided by the text of the Constitution according to its own interpretation of it; and that consequently in the event of irreconcilable interpretations, the prevalence of one or the other department must depend on the nature of the case, as receiving its final decision from the one or the other, and passing from that decision into effect, without involving the functions of any other."[2] What he evidently had in mind was that each

[1] *Writings* (Hunt ed.), vol. VI, p. 349.
[2] Manuscript, *Madison Papers*, Library of Congress.

department should have the final authority to decide questions relating to the exercise of powers within its own sphere of action. The Supreme Court, that is, should have no authority to question the judgment of Congress concerning what would be a valid exercise of legislative power, or of the President concerning an exercise of executive power. The opposite hypothesis, he contended, would establish a judicial oligarchy and destroy the principle of the separation of powers.[1] Furthermore, in the Federal Convention he had even been opposed to giving the Supreme Court a general jurisdiction over cases arising under the Constitution. He "doubted whether it was not going too far to extend the jurisdiction of the court generally to cases arising under the Constitution, and whether it ought not to be limited to cases of a judiciary nature."[2] But this statement, like one or two other assertions of his which have been used by opponents of judicial review to condemn the principle, probably signified nothing more than his fear of an undermining of the separation of powers. If the Court were to have the final word on *every* question of a constitutional nature, there might be some danger that the republican form of government would be perverted into an oligarchy. There is no proof that he had any intention of condemning judicial review as such. It would appear justifiable to conclude then that Madison's conception of judicial review was limited to protection of private rights against impulsive legislatures and to settlement of ordinary

[1] *Annals of Congress*, vol. I, p. 501.

[2] Farrand, *Records of the Federal Convention*, vol. II, p. 430. He also deprecated an all-inclusive power of judicial review in his remarks on Jefferson's Draught of a Constitution for Virginia. *Writings* (Hunt ed.), vol. IX, pp. 284-294.

conflicts between Federal and State authorities. But this was certainly allowing ample jurisdiction to the courts and over the very matters involving the strongest feeling between classes and therefore destined to produce the sharpest controversy.

Two guiding principles influenced Madison in the formulation of his theory of legislative, executive, and judicial powers. The first of these was the principle of the separation of powers, which he regarded as a prime essential of free government and the chief protection against tyranny. Of the three departments he appeared to consider the legislative and the executive the most disposed to self-aggrandizement; the former because of its numerous composition and the indefinite nature of its powers; and the latter because of its management of foreign relations and its control over the military, the two powers of government most easily perverted to the ends of despotism. In order to prevent executive despotism he was inclined to exalt the legislature, especially by according to it a large measure of control over treaties and other matters of foreign policy. To forestall legislative tyranny he endowed the judicial department with the special function of protecting the natural rights of the citizen to life, liberty, and property. And then, finally, to exclude a preponderance of the judiciary, he insisted upon the co-ordinate status of all three branches of the government and denied the right of the courts to overrule another department's interpretation of the extent of its constitutional powers.

The second of the great principles that conditioned Madison's theory of the powers of the three departments was the principle that the Federal Union rested upon a compact among the people in the States which divided the sovereignty in such a way as to confer a definite portion of it upon the general government, reserving the remainder to the States. The authority of Congress and the President, therefore, was automatically limited by the fact that they possessed only enumerated powers. On the other hand, Madison considered the Federal Supreme Court the appropriate organ for the settlement of ordinary conflicts between Federal and State authorities. He maintained, however, that in the last resort neither the Supreme Court nor any other agency of the general government should have the final authority to interpret the constitutional compact; that right should appertain solely to the parties to the compact themselves, in other words, to the people in the States.

SEVEN

# Conclusion

## SUMMARY

IN concluding this study it may be appropriate first of all to recapitulate briefly the principal doctrines of Madison's political philosophy.

The state as a political society, according to Madison, is an artificial creation of its own members, the result of an agreement, not the product of history or evolution. Its basis is a political compact by which the members agree one with another to submit to the will of the majority, to establish a government, and to surrender to that government some of their sovereign powers. The compact is entered into in the first place because of the uncertainty and injustice of the state of nature. Men are usually governed by selfish purposes and are constantly prone to oppress one another and to unite into factions for their own advantage. The only parties to the compact are the people themselves, acting either as individuals or as separate communities; the government is never a party to the compact but a creature of it.

Before the formation of the political compact, sovereignty inheres in each individual or group of individuals that is to become a party to it. They can divide their sovereign powers as they see fit; sovereignty is not indivisible or inalienable. But however the division may be made the parties to the compact retain their natural rights to life, liberty, and property, and also the ultimate right of revolution if absolutely necessary to the preservation of their natural rights.

The primary purpose of government is to protect the divergent faculties of men in acquiring property. The principal task of legislation is to regulate the various and conflicting economic interests. "That alone is a just government which impartially secures to every man whatever is his own." Property, however, includes not only external possessions, but also the liberty and safety of a man's person, his knowledge and opinions, and the right to the free use of his talents.

To be considered anywhere nearly perfect, a state must embody the following characteristics: an agrarian basis, but with enough development of other economic interests to provide some degree of self-sufficiency; republicanism, that is, elective and representative government, as distinguished from monarchy or pure democracy; federalism, to avoid both the tyrannical propensities of unitary government and the "imbecilities" of the confederate form; the separation of powers, which is the safest guaranty against despotism; and, most important of all, an extended sphere of government so that the citizens will be broken up into so large a number of diverse interests that no one faction or combination of factions can ever rule the state.

Since there are natural laws that operate in the social and economic spheres, the province of government should be carefully restricted. It is not the business of government to promote prosperity or to prevent poverty, but rather to provide a *milieu* of confidence, justice, and security in which every citizen can garner the rewards of his industry, economy, and talent. Nevertheless, the government may suitably engage in the construction of railroads and highways, and may levy protective tariffs in order to promote the national security and to preserve a due balance among agriculture, industry, and commerce.

While sovereignty resides in the members of the state and is expressed through the will of the majority, there is no absolute right of the majority to govern as it pleases. All government is limited by the fundamental concepts of a higher law of abstract justice and universal reason. A despotism of many is just as reprehensible as a despotism of one or of a few. Effectual safeguards must therefore be erected against the absolute rule of majorities. Among the most desirable are the following: a system of checks and balances; a system of representation to refine and enlarge the public views; an extension of the territorial sphere of government to prevent a common sentiment from ever being felt by a majority of the people; fairly long terms for members of the legislature; and, above all, a Senate with sufficient reputation for wisdom and virtue to curb the violent impulses of the masses. At the same time it is essential to prevent domination of the government by a minority. Accordingly, some agencies of the government should be chosen by direct popular election, and adoption or amendment of the fundamental law by less than a majority of the people should be rendered impossible.

The right of suffrage is a necessary provision in a republican constitution, and on general principles it should be widely distributed. Nevertheless, no apportionment of the franchise can ever justly be made that will result in the infringement of the rights of liberty and property. If the vote be allowed equally to all, the indigent masses will probably succumb to envy and force the enactment of unjust laws against the more prosperous minority. The suffrage cannot be restricted, however, to those who own property, lest the rights of persons be infringed. Some means ought to be devised whereby the interests of both persons and property can be represented. It would be meet, therefore, that a universal franchise should prevail for the election of one branch of the legislature, with a property franchise for the other.

The republican ideal must embrace opposition to hereditary privilege, a belief in the equality of all men as human beings, and the highest regard for individual rights. The existence of slavery is incompatible with this ideal, and no republican constitution should recognize property in human beings. Guaranties of freedom of speech, of religion and the press, trial by jury, exemption from unlawful searches and seizures, and the other natural rights which are reserved when the political compact is entered into are the prime requisites of free government. To a certain extent it is desirable to embody them in a formal declaration or bill of rights, although there is the danger that such a declaration may not be interpreted with sufficient latitude, with the result that a definite enumeration of rights may provide a pretext for the violation of other rights not enumerated. But whether a bill of rights is drawn up or not, these essential elements of the law of nature constitute an absolute limitation upon the powers of government which neither the legislature nor any other agency can modify or evade.

The chief corroding principle of republican government is war, which promotes corruption, encourages despotism, and destroys liberty. Wars should be made unpopular by compelling the generations that fight them to pay for them, rather than allowing them to shift the burden to future generations. Furthermore, militarism, a main germinator of war, should never be allowed to take root in a republican system. Standing armies should be avoided as a curse, and the military should be kept strictly subordinated to the civil authority.

The United States is a true political society, a state, having a government of sovereign powers, and is not a mere league or confederation of independent units. Like all other political societies the American Union rests upon a compact among its members by which they agreed one with another to abide permanently by the will of the majority, save in extreme cases involving the natural right of self-preservation. This compact is the Constitution of the United States, the parties to which are the States themselves, that is, the people in them as sovereign communities. The people in the States, the original sovereigns in this country when the Constitution was adopted, agreed with each other to establish a central government and to surrender some of their sovereign powers to it. By so doing they created a new body politic in exactly the same way as individuals in a state of nature set up a government over themselves and endow it with sovereign powers for the greater security of their natural rights.

The Constitution of the United States has in several ways a unique character. In the first place, it is not only a compact, but it is also a law which the courts, both national and local, are bound to enforce. In the second place, it contains as a cardinal principle a division of sovereignty between the States in their united and in their individual capacities, so that the government of the Union is made just as truly sovereign within the sphere of its powers as are the particular States within their respective spheres. Finally, the Constitution is unique in that it provides for a political system which is neither wholly national nor wholly federal. So far as its foundation and the derivation and extent of its powers are concerned, it is both federal and national, mainly the former, but in respect of the operation of its powers it is entirely national, since the powers of both the central and local governments operate directly upon individuals.]

Since the people in the States, in dividing the sovereignty, made the general government a government of enumerated powers only, it follows that the Constitution of the United States should be strictly construed. The general government can exercise only those powers that are actually granted to it and such others as may be absolutely necessary to carry them into execution. Under no conditions may the Federal authority be allowed to possess inherent powers or powers derived from a supposed common law of the United States, however logical or necessary they may appear to be.

The two provisions of the Constitution most liable to a dangerous construction are the necessary and proper clause and the general welfare clause. The former does not mean that Congress can employ any means appropriate for, or conducive to, the execution of one of the enumerated powers, and not expressly prohibited. "Necessary" means really necessary. To construe it otherwise would be to destroy the essential character of the Federal government as a government of limited powers and to reduce the reserved powers of the States to a nullity. For there is hardly any conceivable act of Congress which could not be considered an appropriate means adapted to some end provided for in the Constitution.

The general welfare clause is only an introductory expression and was never intended to be a grant of power of any sort. Its meaning must be sought in the succeeding enumeration of powers in the Constitution, or else the general government of this country is a consolidated government of absolute power. If Congress can expend money for any purpose alleged to be for the general welfare, then there are practically no limits to the Federal authority. Even religion, education, and the protection of life and property in the States would be brought within the scope of this authority. The only proper interpretation of this clause, therefore, is that Federal taxation shall be for some particular purpose, embraced within one of the enumerated powers, and conducive to the general welfare.

On the other hand, the Constitution is not to be construed with the rigidity of a penal statute. Not all powers are to be regarded as prohibited to the Federal government which are not expressly granted in the Constitution. Certain powers by implication must also be admitted; otherwise many of the enumerated powers could not be carried into execution. It is necessary, for example, that Congress should have authority to encourage navigation and shipbuilding and to retaliate, even to the extent of protective tariffs, against the trade discriminations of other countries as essential means of regulating foreign commerce. Furthermore, in certain cases not clearly provided for in the written Constitution, repeated recognitions of the validity of certain acts, over a considerable period of time, by the different branches of the national government, by the

States, and by the general will of the people may be sufficient to establish their constitutionality.

Since the Constitution is a compact, it is binding upon all the States just as much as a contract between individuals is binding upon all who are parties to it. No one of them by unilateral action has any right to disregard it. The Constitution, however, is more than a mere agreement among sovereign States: it is a compact establishing a political society and dividing the sovereignty between the government of that society and the States who are the members of it. Only the States collectively have any authority to construe the division of sovereignty. It follows that no individual State has the right to nullify an act of the general government.

The States collectively, however, most certainly do have the right to "interpose" for the preservation of the original division of sovereignty. That is, in case of any encroachments or usurpations by the general government, they have the right and the duty to co-operate in arresting the progress of the evil, not by violent action but by the peaceful methods of securing amendments to the Constitution, changing the representation in Congress, initiating impeachments, or appealing to the Federal judiciary.

If the individual State has no authority to nullify an act of the general government, even less does it have the right to secede from the Union. The political compact can only be dissolved by the consent of all the parties to it, or at least by a majority of them. The States are not completely sovereign units, as under a league or confederation, but they are members of a body politic which no one of them can have the right to destroy. But while there is no *constitutional* right of secession, each State must be admitted to possess a *natural* right to withdraw from the compact in the face of conditions absolutely intolerable, just as the individual may expatriate himself or go into exile when the oppressions of political society have become unbearable.

The three departments of government under the Constitution are co-ordinate, and care must be taken to prevent the preponderance of one or another. This co-ordinate character implies the ultimate right of each department to determine the scope of its own constitutional authority in relation to the other departments. It implies also that the function of interpreting the Constitution must not be a monopoly of the judiciary. The legislative and executive branches have at least a qualified power to decide questions of constitutionality in cases not explicitly covered in the organic law, to the extent of confirming repeated recognitions of the validity of some doubtful issue.

To the legislative department belong all powers of a distinctly law-making character, including the power to determine all questions relating to the disposition of the United States in regard to peace or war and the power to approve or reject all treaties that have anything of the nature of laws. The President and the Senate must not be permitted to usurp legislative functions through an exercise of the treaty-making power. While the legislative branch has a tendency to draw everything into its "impetuous vortex," the veto power of the executive is a sufficient check against an abuse of this tendency.

The primary function of the executive department is to take care that the laws be faithfully executed. It is not its business to legislate. Hence the veto power should not be used in the prospective mode to force the enactment of laws against the will of the legislature. On the other hand, in matters of administration the President must be allowed freedom from Congressional interference. Congress has no right to limit the tenure of office of Presidential appointees, nor has the Senate any right to control over the removal power of the President. An essential means of executing the laws is the power to discipline subordinates, and the removal power is a necessary incident to such discipline. The chief danger of executive tyranny lies in the President's control over foreign relations and military affairs. Extreme care should therefore be taken to prevent any enlargement of the President's discretionary authority in respect of these matters.

The Federal judiciary, by reason of its composition and the gravity and deliberation of its proceedings, is the department of government to which the right of expounding the Constitution most logically appertains. But this function does not belong exclusively to the courts. Since the three departments are co-ordinate, the legislature and the executive, in the exercise of their respective functions, have authority to decide what the Constitution means in doubtful cases, and this authority is not subject to review by the courts where any conflict between departments over the limits of their authority is involved.

The chief functions of the Federal courts are to preserve the original division of sovereignty between the central government and the States, to decide controversies of a judicial nature arising under the Constitution, and to protect the private rights of individuals from impulsive and unjust laws. It is the business of the courts, in other words, to uphold the ideal of limited government, to enforce the limitations contained in the Constitution and in the general body of abstract rights. This does not mean an unqualified authority of judicial review. The States as parties to the constitutional compact cannot be deprived of their ultimate right to take collective action by peaceful means against Federal violations of the division of sovereignty, nor can the sacred principle of the separation of powers be sacrificed to judicial supremacy.

### THE SOURCES OF MADISON'S PHILOSOPHY

The sources of a political philosopher's ideas always constitute a discouraging subject of inquiry, for the products of the mind are not units of definite constituency that can be exchanged and acquired like bars of gold or parcels of land. What appear to be identical ideas in the writings of two philosophers may serve altogether different purposes or possess a different value and import and may have been evolved by each thinker independently. Furthermore, doctrines that have become the intellectual property of an age may decidedly influence a philosopher without his being conscious of the source of that influence—and even if he were conscious of it, he would not necessarily proclaim the fact.

These difficulties are no less real in the case of Madison's ideas than is true generally. It is still possible, however, to determine the origin of a good many of his theories. In a few instances he actually mentioned the source from which a particular doctrine was derived. In other cases the resemblance between his teachings and those of some other great thinker is entirely too striking to admit the possibility of mere coincidence.

First among the intellectual forebears of Madison may be mentioned the Englishman, James Harrington, whose

*Commonwealth of Oceana* was published in 1656. In this work Harrington set forth a theory of the economic basis of politics which definitely foreshadowed that of *Federalist* Number 10. The form and character of government, he argued, result from the mode of distribution of property: "Such as is the proportion or balance of dominion or property in land, such is the nature of the empire."[1] Furthermore, he maintained that factions and parties in a state arise from the uneven distribution of wealth, which sets groups and classes of men in perpetual conflict, "the one party endeavoring to preserve their eminence and inequality, and the other to attain to inequality."[2] Madison's theory of the basis of government and the origin of factions differed only in being more explicit.

The remedies which Harrington proposed for government by faction were not identical with those recommended by Madison, but they were not so dissimilar either. He suggested a system of popular election with ample provision for rotation in office as one means of curbing the evil. He recommended also an agrarian law imposing a limit on the amount of land any one person could hold.[3] It will be recalled that Madison also contended that property should not be too unevenly distributed. Both men, however, seemed to believe that a design of government to prevent any interest or combination of interests from becoming too powerful should be the chief reliance. Harrington avowed that "The perfection of government lies upon such a libration in the frame of it that no man or men in or under it can have the interest, or having the

[1] *Commonwealth of Oceana* (Morley ed.), London, 1887, p. 18.
[2] *Ibid.*, p. 39.
[3] *Ibid.*, p. 40.

interest, can have the power to disturb it with sedition."[1] The relation between this and Madison's idea of extending the territorial sphere of government so that the number of interests would be so great that no combination of them could ever form a majority appears fairly obvious.

Certain other doctrines of Harrington show a definite correspondence with theories of Madison, whether or not there was any direct connection. For example, Harrington deprecated the idea of a commonwealth ruled by "mechanics," who would be so engrossed in the business of earning a living that they would not have the leisure or the inclination to study the public interest.[2] He believed in the sovereignty of the people limited by conceptions of universal right and justice, with a written constitution as a fundamental law embodying at least some of these limitations. He believed in a legislature having a continuous existence, divided into two branches, with one branch more numerous than the other. And, last of all, he advocated the principle of the separation of powers into legislative, executive, and judicial as a primary means of preventing despotic rule.[3]

The English philosopher who influenced Madison the most was undoubtedly John Locke, but whether directly or indirectly is open to debate. It is conceivable, although not probable, that Madison had not read very much of Locke; he mentioned him only once in any of his writings.[4]

[1] *Ibid.*, p. 37.

[2] *Ibid.*, p. 150.

[3] Theodore W. Dwight, "Harrington and His Influence upon American Political Institutions and Political Thought," *Political Science Quarterly*, vol. II (1887), pp. 1-24.

[4] Letters of Helvidius, No. 1, *Writings* (Hunt ed.), vol. VI, p. 144.

It may be that nearly all of his knowledge of Lockian principles was derived second hand from other Americans, especially Jefferson, who were disciples of the great champion of the Glorious Revolution of 1688. But whatever the immediate sources of that knowledge, it was certainly extensive. An amazing number of Madison's cardinal theories duplicated those of Locke even in minor particulars. Others that were elaborated into something original rested squarely upon Lockian foundations.

To begin with, Madison advanced a theory of property virtually identical with that of Locke. In his note to the speech of August 7, 1787, on the suffrage, he avowed it to be a principle of natural law that an individual has an exclusive right to those portions of land with which he incorporates his labor and improvements.[1] Likewise Madison's conception of the object of government as the protection of property was a repetition, conscious or unconscious, of Locke's contention that "the great and chief end of men uniting into commonwealths and putting themselves under government, is the preservation of their property."[2] And just as Locke gave to the word "property" the meaning of "life, liberty, and estate,"[3] Madison inclined at times toward a like interpretation.

In similar fashion Madison's theories of the foundation of political society were undoubtedly derived from Locke. Both men believed in a pre-political state of nature in which each individual had absolute dominion over his

[1] *Documentary History of the Constitution*, vol. V, p. 444; compare Locke, *Two Treatises of Civil Government* (Everyman ed.), p. 131.

[2] *Two Treatises of Civil Government*, p. 180.

[3] *Ibid.*, p. 180.

person and possessions and an unlimited right to enforce their protection. They believed that the state was formed because of the inconveniences and insecurity arising from the fact of every man's being a judge in his own cause. To remedy this condition of uneasiness men agreed with one another to form a body politic and to establish a government, surrendering to it their natural right of protecting their persons and property, or in other words yielding to it the power to enforce the law of nature.[1]

Such a theory of the origin of the state clearly implied a conception of sovereignty as alienable and divisible. According to the Lockian view, which Madison accepted, sovereignty originally inhered in the people as individuals. In order to increase their own security, they surrendered a portion of sovereignty to the government which they united in establishing. But all that they surrendered was the power to enforce their natural rights to life, liberty, and property; the remainder of their original sovereignty they retained for themselves. Under no circumstances did they endow the government with absolute authority in all cases whatsoever.[2]

The conclusion was therefore inescapable that the powers of government were limited, that its authority could extend only so far as to secure everyone's person and property against those defects that made the state of nature so unsafe and uneasy. The great body of abstract rights constituted a higher law which no government, regardless of its form, could transgress. If it made any attempt to take away or destroy the property of the people, or to reduce them to slavery under arbitrary power, the people were absolved

[1] *Supra*, pp. 30-31; Locke, *op. cit.*, pp. 160-66.

[2] *Supra*, pp. 34-35; Locke, *op. cit.*, pp. 179-188.

from any further obedience to it, and had the right to return to their original liberty, or to set up a new government conducive to the ends of political society. The law of nature stood as an eternal rule to all who held the public trust; the decrees which they made for other men's actions had to be conformable to that law, or else they had no validity.[1]

The government, then, according to both Madison and Locke, was the creature of the political compact and the executive of the law of nature. It was not itself a party to the compact, and therefore had no rights under it, not even to determine the scope of its own powers. The people as the sole parties to the compact alone had final authority to construe it and to judge in the event of its violation. In case of a controversy between the government and some of the people, the majority of the people had the ultimate right to decide.[2]

Madison's theory of the Union was essentially nothing but a refinement of this general theory of the foundation of the state, conceived in Lockian terms. That is, he made the people, incorporated as political communities, the original sovereigns, who had agreed with one another to form a Union, to establish a general government, and to surrender a portion of their sovereignty to it, reserving the remainder to themselves. The general government was therefore a government of limited power, defined in the constitutional compact which provided for the division of sovereignty. The people in the States, as the only parties to that compact, had the final right to construe it; but only by collective action, that is, by the action of the majority.

[1] *Supra,* pp. 34-35; Locke, *op. cit.,* pp. 184-85, 228-29.

[2] *Supra,* pp. 122-23; Locke, *op. cit.,* pp. 241-42.

No individual State had the right to impose its construction upon all of the others, to judge, for example, when the compact had been violated by the general government. No individual State, therefore, had the right to nullify the acts of the general government, or to secede from the Union, except in cases of intolerable oppression, when a State would have the same right as an individual to withdraw from the body politic for self-preservation.[1]

Madison would seem to have been indebted in some degree to Locke for his theory of legislative and executive powers. The English philosopher taught that the legislative was the supreme organ of government, "for what can give laws to another must needs be superior to him," and that the executive and federative branches were distinctly subordinate. Even the "prerogative" which he allowed to the executive was mainly a discretionary power to supplement the legislative authority, by adding to or setting aside laws when necessary for the public good.[2] Madison also admitted a natural pre-eminence of the legislative branch because of the indefinite character of its powers, but he was rather inclined to deplore that pre-eminence instead of justifying it as did Locke. Nevertheless, in spite of his fears of legislative usurpations of power, he never proposed executive domination as a remedy. He was disposed to look rather to the judiciary for protection against excesses of legislative power, especially where violations of private rights were involved, and he usually denied to the executive any discretionary authority.[3]

Madison's doctrine of judicial power owed comparatively

[1] *Supra*, pp. 121-24.
[2] *Op. cit.*, pp. 193-99.
[3] *Supra*, pp. 138-39.

little to the English source of so much of the rest of his theory. Locke did not commit himself definitely to a principle of judicial review, even for the purpose of protecting individual rights. The following passage was his only reference to the subject: "And so, whoever has the legislative or supreme power of any commonwealth, is bound to govern by established standing laws, promulgated and known to the people, and not by extemporary decrees; by indifferent and upright judges, who are to decide controversies by those laws."[1] Although the meaning of the foregoing passage is not altogether clear, it is quite possible that the author intended that the judges should interpose in some manner against arbitrary and unjust laws, perhaps by refusing to apply them in individual cases. The theory of judicial control in this country, however, in the form accepted by the fathers of the Constitution, was the product primarily of the influence of Coke and of the special historical circumstances growing out of the relations between the colonies and the mother country, although Locke's emphasis upon the substantive rights of the individual as an automatic restraint upon the powers of the legislature cannot be ignored.[2]

The only Frenchman who seems to have influenced the development of Madison's philosophy very much was Montesquieu; but his influence was great enough to compensate the lack thereof from others of the same nationality. Moreover, Madison acknowledged his intellectual debt to Montesquieu, not as fully as he might have done, but enough to indicate the high esteem in which he held the baron's

[1] *Op. cit.*, p. 182.
[2] *Supra*, pp. 147-48.

work.[1] In fact, Henry Jones Ford maintained that Montesquieu's teachings were more influential in America than they ever were in his own country,[2] although such a conclusion would appear a bit doubtful in view of the fact that the French Constitution of 1791 was based directly upon those teachings.

Nevertheless, Montesquieu's chief work, *The Spirit of the Laws*, did certainly contain a number of doctrines that bore a positive resemblance to the theories of Madison and consequently to much of the substance of the American Constitution. Among them were the following: the great ideal of political society is stability or permanence, and the agency most baneful to that ideal is the spirit of faction;[3] there is a natural law of justice antecedent and superior to the positive law;[4] in a well-ordered republic the divisions of land ought to be small and substantially equal,[5] but the principle of popular government is corrupted, not only when the spirit of equality is extinct, but also when the people fall into a spirit of extreme equality, "when each citizen would fain be upon a level with those whom he has chosen to command him."[6]

The element in Montesquieu's philosophy which chiefly influenced Madison was the theory of the separation of powers. The eminent baron contended that there is a disposition in man to abuse any extent of power that may be

[1] *Federalist* (Lodge ed.), No. 47, pp. 300-3.

[2] *The Rise and Growth of American Politics*, p. 29.

[3] Baron de Montesquieu, *The Spirit of the Laws*, new edition, revised by J. V. Prichard, two volumes, London, 1909, vol. I, pp. 21-22.

[4] *Ibid.*, vol. I, p. 2.

[5] *Ibid.*, vol. I, p. 49.

[6] *Ibid.*, vol. I, p. 119.

entrusted to him, and that "to prevent this abuse it is necessary from the very nature of things that power should be a check to power."[1] He avowed that in every government there are three types of power—the legislative, the executive, and the judicial, and he maintained that when any two or more of these are united in the same person, liberty is at an end.[2] The correspondence between these doctrines and Madison's views regarding the evil propensities of man's nature and a fusion of governmental powers as "the very definition of tyranny" needs only to be mentioned.[3]

Montesquieu marked out in some detail the prescriptions for a system of checks and balances designed to make the separation of powers fulfill its intended purpose. He recommended, first of all, that the executive should be endowed with a veto power, in order that he might restrain the encroachments of the legislature. Without this check he maintained that the legislative would soon destroy the other powers.[4] In the second place, he recommended that the legislative body should have the power of impeachment, the charge to be brought by the lower house and the trial to be conducted by the upper house.[5] Finally, he advised that the two houses of the legislature should have the power to check the actions of each other "by the mutual privilege of rejecting."[6] The system would thus be complete. Each house would have the power to curb the usurpations of the

[1] *Ibid.*, vol. I, p. 161.
[2] *Ibid.*, vol. I, pp. 162-63.
[3] *Supra*, p. 41.
[4] *Op. cit.*, vol. I, p. 169.
[5] *Ibid.*, vol. I, p. 171.
[6] *Ibid.*, vol. I, p. 171.

other. The legislature as a whole would be checked by the veto power of the executive. And the executive in turn would be restrained by the threat of impeachment and by the legislative right to examine the manner in which its laws were being executed.[1] The reader will recall that this was almost exactly the system of checks and balances recommended by Madison and embodied in the Constitution, save for the addition of the legislative power to override an executive veto.[2]

On the other hand, it should not be forgotten that there was a good deal in *The Spirit of the Laws* which Madison did not adopt, and some which he must have abominated. Montesquieu, for example, preferred monarchy as the best form of government[3] and believed that there should be an hereditary nobility with the power of rejecting legislation.[4] He thought that a republic could exist only with a small territory.[5] He considered bills of attainder justifiable deprivations of the liberty of individuals "in order to preserve it for the whole community."[6] Lastly, although he condemned slavery in principle, he justified negro slavery on the ground that the members of the black race were not human beings.[7]

Probably the political philosopher who influenced Madison the most was not a European at all, but Jefferson, one of his own contemporaries in this country. The two

NB

[1] *Ibid.*, vol. I, pp. 169-71.
[2] *Supra*, pp. 41-42.
[3] *Op. cit.*, vol. I, pp. 59-60.
[4] *Ibid.*, vol. I, p. 167.
[5] *Ibid.*, vol. I, p. 130.
[6] *Ibid.*, vol. I, p. 214.
[7] *Ibid.*, vol. I, p. 257.

men were close friends and associates in political life for more than fifty years. They carried on a voluminous correspondence on political questions, and Madison, who was eight years younger than Jefferson, frequently asked the latter for advice. They appear to have read about the same books and to have had similar intellectual interests. In addition to their association for eight years in the management of executive affairs of the Federal government, they were leaders for an even longer period of the same political party; and when Jefferson retired from the Presidency he designated Madison to succeed him.

In view of these circumstances one would naturally expect that the two men would have held a good many political ideas in common. Such was indeed the case to an extent not commonly realized. Jefferson believed as firmly as did Madison in the origin of the state through a political compact among individuals, the original sovereigns, who by that compact established a government and surrendered to it the power to enforce their natural rights.[1] Both regarded government as a necessary evil and feared despotism as the greatest of all vices.[2] Although professing their devotion to popular rule, both denied the absolute sovereignty of the majority and recommended the separation of powers and a system of checks and balances in order to prevent despotism, including the despotism of the majority.[3] Both distrusted the mobs of great cities and favored an agrarian basis for the American republic.[4] Both enter-

[1] *Writings of Jefferson* (Ford ed.), vol. X, pp. 32ff.

[2] *Ibid.*, vol. II, p. 224; *supra*, pp. 47, 75.

[3] *Ibid.*, vol. II, p. 224; *supra*, pp. 41-43.

[4] *Writings of Jefferson* (Washington ed.), vol. I, p. 403; *supra*, p. 36.

tained the same conceptions of the Union and of nullification and secession; at least Madison contended that such was the case.[1] Jefferson agreed with, if he did not inspire, Madison's views of constitutional construction, especially of the general welfare and necessary and proper clauses.[2] Jefferson also subscribed to theories of judicial review and executive power similar to those of Madison.[3] Finally, both men condemned slavery in principle, abhorred monarchy and hereditary aristocracy, and demanded a strict subordination of the military to the civil authority.[4]

It should be noted, however, that there were elements in Madison's philosophy which were positively not of Jeffersonian origin. He believed in coercive government, hated anarchy almost as much as despotism, and taught that the essence of government is force.[5] The Sage of Monticello, on the other hand, condemned energetic government, avowing that it is always oppressive, and suggested that the ideal condition of man would be a state of affairs approaching pure anarchy, or no government at all.[6] Madison was inclined to be suspicious of human motives, contending that men are generally governed by covetousness, jealousy, and a desire for aggrandizement, and that the masses are especially prone to hatred and envy of the more prosperous minority.[7] As a consequence he was more cautious than Jefferson in advocating the

[1] Notes on Nullification, *Writings* (Hunt ed.), vol. IX, p. 589.
[2] *Writings of Jefferson* (Ford ed.), vol. X, p. 90.
[3] *Ibid.*, vol. X, pp. 160-61.
[4] *Ibid.*, vol. IX, p. 477; vol. IV, p. 426; *supra*, pp. 76-85.
[5] *Supra*, pp. 43-45.
[6] *Writings of Jefferson* (Ford ed.), vol. IV, pp. 362, 479.
[7] *Supra*, pp. 30-31, 65.

right of self-government. Madison denounced pure democracy as one of the worst forms of government; he believed that the sentiments of the people should be refined and enlarged by elected representatives, particularly by a Senate composed of men of wisdom and virtue; and he did not favor Jefferson's cherished idea of periodic renewals of constitutions, and laws.[1]

Furthermore, Madison's emphasis upon the sanctity of property rights and his doctrine of the economic basis of politics did not come from Jefferson; neither did his elaborate scheme for preventing class rule by splitting the population into so great a number of conflicting interests that no combination of them could ever form a majority.[2] He displayed also a greater interest in promotion of commerce and manufactures by the government than did Jefferson. Both men had natural prepossessions in favor of a republic of small freeholders, but Madison was deeply concerned, especially in his later years, with the problem of national self-sufficiency, and he considered a policy of protectionism necessary to speed up the development of industry.[3]

There were doubtless other sources of Madison's theory than those already discussed, but they are not so easy to determine. He mentioned Aristotle only once,[4] and Plato, Cicero, Machiavelli, and Rousseau not at all, and

[1] *Supra*, pp. 68-70.

[2] *Supra*, pp. 38-39.

[3] *Supra*, pp. 52-57.

[4] In a half-finished essay on The Influence of Domestic Slavery on Government, he referred to Aristotle's doctrine that the citizen should be free from private cares so as to devote himself exclusively to public service. Manuscript, *Madison Papers*, Library of Congress.

probably owed very little to any of them directly. He was a profound student of ancient, medieval, and early modern constitutions, especially those of confederacies, and he profited at least from a knowledge of their deficiencies.[1] There is evidence that he was thoroughly familiar with the works of Plutarch, Demosthenes, Grotius, Coke, Diderot, and the Abbé Mably,[2] but how much he may have been influenced by them is another question. For his theories of international relations he drew copiously from Vattel, Pufendorf, and Bynkershoek,[3] and it is quite possible that their emphasis upon a higher law of justice and right reason may have affected his thinking.

The foregoing analysis of sources is by no means intended to convey the impression that Madison's political philosophy was a mere synthetic concoction made up of assorted products of the minds of other sages. Such a conclusion would be neither fair nor accurate. Madison probably made just about as many original contributions to political theory as any other American of his time, not excluding Jefferson. Among these original contributions may be mentioned, first of all, the doctrine that the geographic sphere of government must be of considerable extent, so that the population will be broken up into so many diverse interests that no combination of them can ever gain control of the state. Harrington had already maintained the necessity of some organization of government adapted to prevent the rule of factions, but it was left to Madison to work out a practicable scheme for the attainment of that purpose.

[1] *Federalist* (Lodge ed.), Nos. 18, 19, 20, pp. 102-19.

[2] *Writings* (Hunt ed.), vol. II, p. 43; Hunt, *Life of Madison*, p. 114.

[3] *Writings* (Hunt ed.), vol. VII, pp. 204-375.

Another of Madison's original achievements was his theory of federalism, which was totally different from the principles upon which historic confederations had been based. This theory included a number of cardinal elements: first, the establishment of a political society, a Union composed of a number of subdivisions as distinct political communities; second, a division of sovereignty between the Union and the individual subdivisions as political communities; third, a government of the Union derived in part from the governments of the subdivisions, and in part from the people themselves; and fourth, and most important of all, the individual citizens as the subjects of both the general government and the governments of the local units—that is, the general government would not be the mere agent of the local governments, dependent upon them for the execution of its powers, but would have authority to operate directly upon the individual citizens of the whole society. It was this last element which most truly distinguished Madison's federalism from all others and was perhaps his greatest contribution to the structure of the American system. He was, however, not the sole originator of this idea. Various others who favored a government of greater energy than the Articles of Confederation provided had advocated it at least tentatively, notably Alexander Hamilton in arguing the case of Rutgers *v.* Waddington and John Jay in his report to Congress as Secretary of Foreign Affairs. But most of these earlier proposals applied primarily to such things as the enforcement of treaties and the punishment of counterfeiting and piracy, and would still have left the central government largely dependent upon the States for the execution of its domestic powers.[1] It was left for Madison to work out the plan for a balanced adjustment in which the Federal government would have authority to act directly upon individuals in every essential sphere, and yet without destroying the sovereignty of the States.

As indicated several times already, Madison's theory of the foundation of the state was derived from Locke. Both men held identical conceptions of the origin of political society through a compact among discrete sovereigns who agreed to be bound by the will of the majority, to establish a government, and to surrender to it the power to enforce the law of nature. But Madison gave to this theory an original variation of great significance. In applying it to the foundation of the American Union he made the people in the States, as organized communities, not as individuals, the ultimate sovereigns and parties to the compact, and thereby evolved a conception of the United States as a true political society with sovereign powers and not a mere confederacy. At the same time he avoided the necessity of annihilating the sovereignty of the States, for like any other parties to a political compact they would retain all that portion of sovereignty which had not been expressly surrendered.

[1] Corwin, "The Progress of Constitutional Theory between the Declaration of Independence and the Meeting of the Philadelphia Convention," *American Historical Review,* vol. XXX, p. 532. Franklin's famous Albany Plan of 1754 also implied a considerable degree of direct authority of the central government over individuals, but chiefly in the military sphere and in the matter of relations with the Indians. Corwin, *The Doctrine of Judicial Review,* pp. 115-16.

## THE SIGNIFICANCE AND INFLUENCE OF MADISON'S THEORY

What should be said of the significance of Madison's political philosophy? It has been variously interpreted. The usual practice has been to regard it as a philosophy of conservatism, an expression of the reactionary movement that developed in the 1780's against the radicalism of the Revolutionary period.[1] By an interesting contrast, however, Daniel De Leon considered Madison's theory as a kind of forerunner of the *Communist Manifesto* because of its emphasis upon the class conflict as the basic force underlying all political action.[2]

The correct view would seem to lie somewhere between these two extremes. Madison was no radical. Firmly as he believed in the class struggle and in economic determinism in the sphere of politics, it is ridiculous to think of him as a kind of John the Baptist to Karl Marx. For the Father of the American Constitution was almost everything that Marx was not. He was a staunch individualist. He was as zealous a champion of private property and private enterprise as any English Whig. And while it is true that he foresaw more clearly than anyone else in his time the pressure of increased population upon the means of subsistence, the concentration of wealth in the hands of a few, and the growth of an enormous class of wage earners without property and without any hope of acquiring it, he did

[1] Merriam, *American Political Theories*, pp. 101-22; Parrington, *op. cit.*, vol. I, pp. 280-88.

[2] *James Madison and Karl Marx*, pamphlet published by the National Executive Committee of the Socialist Labor Party, New York, 1920, pp. 16-18.

not urge a frank acceptance of the class war, and he did not preach the desirability of a triumph of the proletariat over those who live by owning. On the contrary he deplored class antagonism as destructive of the very foundations of stable and orderly government, and he believed that a principal object of statecraft should be to devise means of preventing the domination of any particular interest or group of interests over the whole society.

At the same time Madison's philosophy was not the conservative counterpart of Revolutionary radicalism. In truth, there were very few of the doctrines proclaimed by John Hancock, Samuel Adams, Thomas Paine, and Thomas Jefferson which Madison did not accept. He was in perfect agreement with their theories of natural rights, popular sovereignty, limited government, the separation of powers, and hatred of monarchy and hereditary aristocracy. Practically the only difference between his views and theirs consisted in his rejection of their demands for annual elections, and in his tendency to emphasize property rights rather than personal rights somewhat more heavily than did Paine and Jefferson.

As a matter of fact the radicalism of the Revolutionary leaders has been considerably exaggerated. Like Madison they were nearly all of them perfectly good disciples of John Locke. They believed in private enterprise, and they had no intention of demanding a redistribution of wealth, much less the abolition of private ownership. John Hancock and Samuel Adams even avowed the chief object of government to be the protection of persons *and property*.[1] In fine, the radicalism of the American Revolution was restricted almost entirely to political objectives;

[1] Merriam, *American Political Theories*, p. 62.

it was not directed toward making any fundamental change in the economic order within the country. This was well attested by the fact that nearly all of the State constitutions adopted during and immediately after the Revolution imposed property qualifications for voting and for holding office.[1]

The conclusion may be safely drawn, then, that as a political philosopher Madison was not so far removed from the majority of his contemporaries. Like them he drew from the common stock of ideas of the seventeenth and eighteenth centuries, the former especially, and developed in consequence a conception of the state as an artificial entity and a theory of government as a necessary evil called into existence for the sole purpose of giving to the individual a greater security of person and possessions. Perhaps he may be said to have occupied a kind of middle ground between Jefferson on the one side and Hamilton on the other, but with his antagonism toward monarchy, hereditary privilege, and British institutions generally, he was decidedly nearer to the former than to the latter.

Madison's influence as a political theorist was tempered by profound cultural and social changes which virtually produced a different world in the early nineteenth century from that which existed before. The Romantic movement, for example, with its emphasis upon history and tradition and the organic character of society, dealt a mortal blow to the theories of the Age of Reason which had regarded the state as an artificial product of agreement. Utilitarianism likewise attacked the very fundamentals of the *Naturrecht* philosophy. Both of these movements originated in Europe but soon exerted their influence in America. More directly, the emergence in this

[1] *Ibid.*, pp. 84-86.

country of an intense nationalism, and the increased class consciousness of the slaveocracy, made more and more difficult the preservation of a delicate balance between the government of the Union and the States. Finally, the rise of extreme democracy, based upon Rousseauist conceptions of the absolute sovereignty of the majority, offered a direct challenge to the theories of law and of popular government that prevailed at the time the American Constitution was adopted.

As a consequence of these factors a good many of Madison's favorite theories were thrown into the discard about 1830, or shortly thereafter. His theory of a division of sovereignty between the States in their united and in their individual capacities was partly eclipsed by the doctrine of indivisible sovereignty as taught by the nationalists and the States' rights extremists. The former maintained that sovereignty belonged entirely to the mass of individuals composing the nation, that none of it inhered in the States. The latter contended that sovereignty vested exclusively in the States, that none of it had ever been or ever could be surrendered to the government of the Union. The acceptance of either of these views necessarily meant the rejection of Madison's theory.[1]

In a similar fashion Madison's ideal of limited government had a difficult time withstanding the force of the democratic dogmas of the Jacksonian Revolution. Madison believed that in so far as anyone should exercise sovereign authority, it should be the majority; but he denied that any agency of government should possess unlimited power. He feared that the tyranny of the masses might

[1] For an exposition of these conflicting views of sovereignty see Merriam, *American Political Theories*, pp. 257-89.

become just as oppressive as the tyranny of a prince. The theory of the Jacksonian Democrats, on the other hand, carried the implication that the voice of the people is the voice of God, that the will of the majority is the criterion of right in the world of politics. The influence of the same theory was responsible for the overthrow of Madison's conception of executive power. He regarded the executive in the main as a mere agent to enforce the will of Congress, with little or no discretionary authority, and no right to use the prerogatives of his office to compel the enactment of legislation. The Jacksonian school exalted the President as the supreme representative of the people's will and introduced the spoils system and the prospective veto as means of augmenting the executive power.[1]

The forces of nationalism eventually doomed most of Madison's theories of constitutional interpretation. Nationalist judges like Marshall and Story rode rough-shod over his doctrine that the powers of Congress under the necessary and proper clause were limited to those "absolutely necessary" for the execution of granted powers and his contention that the general welfare clause did not in itself confer any spending power or any other kind of power upon Congress.[2] The Civil War put an end forever to any possible acceptance of his theory that the States alone had the ultimate authority to construe the constitutional compact, that they could "interpose" by collective action in case of its violation by the Federal government, and that any one of them had a *natural* right to secede in case of intolerable

[1] Henry Jones Ford, *op. cit.*, pp. 246, 262.

[2] McCulloch *v.* Maryland, 4 Wheaton 316 (1819); Joseph Story, *Commentaries on the Constitution of the United States*, Boston, 1858, vol. I, sections 971-80.

oppression. In 1868 the Supreme Court gave legal sanction to the relegation of this theory to oblivion by affirming the organic and indestructible character of the Union.[1]

In other respects, however, Madison's influence as a political philosopher has been by no means inconsiderable. His ideas, more than those of any other man, determined the original character of the Federal Constitution.[2] His famous theory of sovereignty was accepted by the Convention, and in the letter from that body submitting the new instrument of government to Congress the declaration was expressly made that sovereignty had been divided between the Union and the States.[3] This same theory of divided sovereignty was adopted by the Supreme Court in the early cases of Chisholm *v.* Georgia[4] and Ware *v.* Hylton.[5] A few years later Chief Justice Marshall flatly repudiated it in the case of Cohens *v.* Virginia, when he avowed that "The people made the Constitution and the people can unmake it . . . But this supreme and irresistible power to make or unmake resides only in the whole body of the people; not in any subdivision of them."[6] In other words, the national and State governments are mere legatees of *sovereign powers; sovereignty* is vested in neither of them. The only *sovereign* is the people of the whole nation. Marshall's successor, Roger B. Taney, revived the theory of divided sovereignty almost in the precise form taught by Madison, except that he did not

[1] Texas *v.* White, 7 Wallace 700.

[2] Farrand, *The Framing of the Constitution of the United States*, pp. 197-198.

[3] Farrand, *Records of the Federal Convention*, vol. II, p. 666.

[4] 2 Dallas 23 (1793).

[5] 3 Dallas 164 (1796).

[6] 6 Wheaton 264 (1821).

believe in the *natural* rights of the States as an additional limitation upon the sovereignty of the Union.[1] In more recent years the Court has shown a decided preference for Marshall's theory—a preference seldom expressed in so many words, but distinctly implied by the decisions in such cases as Stafford *v.* Wallace,[2] Missouri *v.* Holland,[3] Ponzi *v.* Fessenden,[4] and Brooks *v.* United States.[5] Echoes of the older theory, however, have occasionally been heard. The Court definitely affirmed it in 1870 in the case of Collector *v.* Day,[6] and it was at least implied as late as 1918 in the case of Hammer *v.* Dagenhart.[7]

Madison's belief in the existence of a higher law of reason and justice as an automatic limitation upon the powers of government has also been freely used by American jurists, although of course they have not derived it exclusively from him. Chief Justice Marshall employed it in the case of Fletcher *v.* Peck to protect the vested rights of individuals resulting from a public grant, even if the original transaction had been tainted with fraud.[8] Justice Chase in the case of Calder *v.* Bull avowed that there are certain vital principles of free government, implicit in the nature of the social compact, which restrain the powers of

[1] Ableman *v.* Booth, 21 Howard 138 (1858); Ohio Life Insurance and Trust Co. *v.* Debolt, 16 Howard 231 (1853); Dred Scott *v.* Sandford, 20 Howard 4 (1856).

[2] 258 U. S. 495 (1922).

[3] 252 U. S. 416 (1920).

[4] 258 U. S. 254 (1922).

[5] 267 U. S. 432 (1925).

[6] 11 Wallace 113.

[7] 247 U. S. 251.

[8] 6 Cranch 87 (1810).

all legislatures.[1] Since the Civil War the tendency of the courts has been to make use of one or the other of the due process clauses for the protection of private rights,[2] but the older practice has not yet been altogether discarded. In 1878 in the Sinking Fund Cases the Supreme Court held that "The United States are as much bound by their contract as are individuals. If they repudiate their obligations, it is as much repudiation, with all the wrong and reproach that term implies, as it would be if the repudiator had been a State or a municipality or a citizen."[3] And it may be of some significance that this passage was quoted approvingly by Chief Justice Hughes in the recent case of Perry *v.* United States, although it was not the only basis of his opinion.[4]

In only a few other ways has Madison's influence been a factor of much importance in the political history of our country. His view of the spending power of Congress was adopted by the majority of his successors in the Presidency down to the Civil War.[5] Some of his theories of the Union and the Constitution were appropriated by Andrew Jackson, or by whoever wrote the famous message to South Carolina in 1832. This message proclaimed the Constitution to be a compact, which no one of the States could abrogate without the consent of the others. It was held to be a compact "entered into by the several States and ratified by the people thereof respectively," which

[1] 3 Dallas 271 (1798).

[2] E. S. Corwin, "The Due Process Clause before the Civil War," *Harvard Law Review*, vol. XXIV (1910-11), pp. 366-85; 460-79.

[3] 99 U. S. 700.

[4] 294 U. S. 330 (1935).

[5] E. S. Corwin, *The Twilight of the Supreme Court*, pp. 156-68.

was good Madisonian doctrine, although there was the suggestion also, which Madison would have repudiated, that the Federal government was a party to the compact.[1] The author of the paper even admitted that a State had a *natural* right, in case of "long and intolerable oppression," and after all constitutional remedies had failed, to absolve itself from its obligations to the Union and "appeal to the last resort."[2] Here again were not only Madisonian doctrines, but even Madisonian phrases.

Interesting examples of Madison's influence in our own time are to be found in two recent cases decided by the United States Supreme Court: Myers *v.* United States in 1926, and Humphrey's Executor *v.* United States in 1935. The first case involved the right of the President to remove, without the consent of the Senate, executive officers appointed by him subject to Senatorial confirmation. In presenting the opinion of the Court, Chief Justice Taft adopted as his main reliance the arguments of Madison as a member of the First Congress to the effect that each of the departments of government possesses certain inherent powers which the other departments are forbidden to limit, and that the removal power is essential to an effective control by the President over his subordinates, and therefore is a necessary means to the execution of the laws.[3] The second case was decided by a unanimous vote of the Court partly on the basis of the notable exception which Madison made to the exclusive removal power of the President.

[1] Richardson, *op. cit.*, vol. II, p. 622.

[2] *Ibid.*, vol. II, p. 621. The author appeared to claim, however, that this natural right would not be the right of the State as an organized community, but of the people in the State as individuals.

[3] 272 U. S. 52.

In the famous debate of 1789 in the House he had affirmed his belief that the duties of the Comptroller of the United States partook definitely of a judicial character, and that consequently there might be "strong reasons why an officer of this kind should not hold his office at the pleasure of the Executive branch of the Government." He proposed accordingly that the Comptroller should be appointed for a definite term of years, in order to make him responsible "to the public generally" rather than to any particular branch of the government.[1] In the case referred to, Mr. Justice Sutherland denied the general right of the President to remove a member of the Federal Trade Commission and buttressed his argument by references to Madison's doctrine of the special status of quasi-judicial officers.[2]

Probably it is safe to conclude that the influence of Madison's philosophy has not been in proportion to its value. His theories of sovereignty and of the relation of the States to the Union were historically more valid than those of his opponents, whether rabid nationalists or extreme apostles of States' rights. His conception of judicial review was more reasonable, and less calculated to transform the government into an oligarchy of judges, than the doctrine which has come to prevail. His appreciation of the economic basis of politics was an evidence of discernment and frankness altogether too rare in American public life. And, finally, his attitude toward speculative capitalism, and toward domination of the government by the manipulators of "paper wealth," probably would have been conducive to a healthier economic and political order than that which resulted from the Hamiltonian doctrines.

[1] *Annals of Congress*, vol. I, pp. 611-14.

[2] Humphrey's Executor *v.* United States, 295 U. S. 602.

The merit of his philosophy was perhaps diminished somewhat by his inconsistencies and reversals of attitude. He traveled all the way from a rather extreme nationalism in the early sessions of the Philadelphia Convention to the defense of a modified nullificationism at the end of his career. He adulterated his doctrine of strict construction of the Constitution by preaching the legality of protective tariffs. Although he vied with Jefferson in professing devotion to liberty, he sanctified the property right and emphasized the need for coercive government as a remedy for the depravity of man. He was prone to contradict himself and to shift positions quickly at the command of expediency. In combating monopolization of the treaty-making power by the President and the Senate, he denied that the Constitution bestowed any general discretionary authority upon the executive;[1] but in defending the exclusive removal authority of the President, he maintained that the opening clause of Article II was in itself a grant of power.[2] Most of Madison's shortcomings, however, as a political philosopher probably resulted from the rapidly changing political scene which he had to face, and from the inroads which office-holding made upon his intellectual integrity. Perhaps the number of other men who could have played as active a part in the hurly-burly of events, retaining the while consistency as a crowning virtue, would not have been large.

[1] *Writings* (Hunt ed.), vol. VI, pp. 138ff.

[2] Elliot, *Debates*, vol. IV, pp. 343-44.

# Bibliography

## PRIMARY SOURCES

*American State Papers; Documents, Legislative and Executive, of the Congress of the United States, from the First Session of the First to the Third Session of the Thirteenth Congress, inclusive*, Selected and Edited under the Authority of Congress by Walter Lowrie, Secretary of the Senate, and Matthew S. Clark, Clerk of the House of Representatives, Washington, Gales and Seaton (1832).

*Annals of Congress; Debates and Proceedings of the Congress of the United States, from the First Session of the First Congress to the Second Session of the Fourth Congress, inclusive*, compiled from Authentic Materials, Washington, Gales and Seaton (1834-1849).

*Documentary History of the Constitution of the United States, Derived from the Records, Manuscripts, and Rolls Deposited in the Bureau of Rolls and Library of the Department of State, from 1786 to 1870*, five volumes, Washington, Department of State (1905).

*Documents Illustrative of the Formation of the Union of the American States*, Selected, Arranged, and Indexed by Charles C. Tansill, House Document number 348, Washington, Government Printing Office (1927).

ELLIOTT, JONATHAN, editor, *The Debates, Resolutions, and Other Proceedings, in Conventions, on the Adoption of the Federal Constitution, as Recommended by the General Convention at Philadelphia, on the 17th of September, 1787*, four volumes, Washington, Gales and Seaton (1838).

FARRAND, MAX, editor, *The Records of the Federal Convention of 1787*, three volumes, New Haven, Yale University Press (1911).

FORD, PAUL LEICESTER, editor, *The Writings of Thomas Jefferson*, ten volumes, New York, G. P. Putnam's Sons (1896).

GILPIN, HENRY D., editor, *The Papers of James Madison, Purchased by Order of Congress; Being His Correspondence and Reports of Debates during the Congress of the Confederation, and His Reports of Debates in the Federal Convention; Now Published from the Original Manuscripts Deposited in the Department of State by Direction of the Joint Library Committee of Congress*, three volumes, Washington (1840).

HARRINGTON, JAMES, *The Commonwealth of Oceana*, with an Introduction by Henry Morley, London, G. Routledge and Sons (1887).

HUNT, GAILLARD, editor, *The Writings of James Madison, Comprising His Public Papers and His Private Correspondence, Including Numerous Papers and Documents Now for the First Time Printed*, nine volumes, New York, G. P. Putnam's Sons (1900).

*Letters and Other Writings of James Madison*, Published by Order of Congress, four volumes, Philadelphia, J. B. Lippincott and Co. (1865).

LOCKE, JOHN, *Two Treatises of Civil Government*, Everyman Library Edition, London, J. M. Dent and Sons, New York, E. P. Dutton and Co. (1924).

LODGE, HENRY CABOT, editor, *The Federalist, A Commentary on the Constitution of the United States, Being a Collection of Essays Written in Support of the Constitution Agreed upon September 17, 1787, by the Federal Convention*, New York and London, G. P. Putnam's Sons (1888).

MADISON, JAMES, *Letter to the Rev. Jedidiah Morse, February 26, 1822*, Manuscript in Princeton University Library, Princeton, New Jersey.

———, *Political Observations*, Manuscript dated April 20, 1795, in Columbia University Library, New York.

MONTESQUIEU, BARON DE, *The Spirit of the Laws*, Translated from the French by Thomas Nugent, New Edition Revised by J. V. Prichard, two volumes, London, George Bell and Sons (1909).

Notes of William Pierce on the Federal Convention of 1787, *American Historical Review*, vol. III, pp. 310-34 (1897-98).

*Papers of James Madison*, ninety volumes, Library of Congress, Washington.

*Princeton University Alumni Records*, Compiled by V. Lansing Collins, unpublished, Princeton University, Office of the Secretary, Princeton, New Jersey.

RICHARDSON, JAMES D., editor, *A Compilation of the Messages and Papers of the Presidents, 1789-1897*, Published by Authority of Congress, ten volumes, Washington, Government Printing Office (1896-1899).

STORY, JOSEPH, *Commentaries on the Constitution of the United States*, two volumes, Boston, Little, Brown and Co. (1858).

WASHINGTON, H. A., editor, *The Works of Thomas Jefferson, Being His Autobiography, Correspondence, Reports, Messages, Addresses, and Other Writings, Official and Private*, nine volumes, Washington, Taylor and Maury (1853).

WEBSTER, DANIEL, *Works*, Fifteenth edition, six volumes, Boston, Little, Brown and Co. (1869).

## SECONDARY WORKS

ADAMS, EPHRAIM DOUGLAS, *The Power of Ideals in American History*, New Haven, Yale University Press (1926).

ADAMS, HENRY, *History of the United States during the Administrations of Jefferson and Madison*, nine volumes, New York, Charles Scribner's Sons (1889).

AMBLER, CHARLES H., *Sectionalism in Virginia from 1776 to 1861*, Chicago, University of Chicago Press (1910).

BEARD, CHARLES A., *American Government and Politics*, Fourth edition, New York, The Macmillan Co. (1925).

———, *An Economic Interpretation of the Constitution of the United States*, New York, The Macmillan Co. (1925).

———, *The Economic Origins of Jeffersonian Democracy*, New York, The Macmillan Co. (1915).

———, *The Supreme Court and the Constitution*, New York, The Macmillan Co. (1912).

BEARD, CHARLES A. and MARY R., *The Rise of American Civilization*, two volumes, New York, The Macmillan Co. (1930).

BEVERIDGE, ALBERT J., *Life of John Marshall*, four volumes, Boston and New York, Houghton Mifflin Co. (1919).

BOURNE, E. G., "The Authorship of the Federalist," *American Historical Review*, vol. II, pp. 443-60 (1897).

CHANNING, EDWARD, *A History of the United States*, six volumes, New York, The Macmillan Co. (1912).

CORWIN, EDWARD S., "Due Process of Law before the Civil War," *Harvard Law Review*, vol. XXIV, pp. 366-85; 460-79 (1910-11).

———, *The Doctrine of Judicial Review; Its Legal and Historical Basis and Other Essays*, Princeton, Princeton University Press (1914).

———, "The Higher Law Background of American Constitutional Law," *Harvard Law Review*, vol. XLII, pp. 148-85; 365-409 (1928-29).

———, "The Progress of Constitutional Theory between the Declaration of Independence and the Meeting of the Philadelphia Convention," *American Historical Review*, vol. XXX, pp. 513-36 (1925).

———, *The Twilight of the Supreme Court*, New Haven, Yale University Press (1934).

COX, I. J., "The American Intervention in West Florida," *American Historical Review*, vol. XVII, pp. 290-311 (1911-12).

DAVIDSON, PHILIP G., "Virginia and the Alien and Sedition Laws," *American Historical Review*, vol. XXXVI, pp. 336-42 (1931).

DELEON, DANIEL, *James Madison and Karl Marx*, Pamphlet Published by the National Executive Committee of the Socialist Labor Party, New York (1920).

DODD, WILLIAM E., *Statesmen of the Old South, Or from Radicalism to Conservative Revolt*, New York, The Macmillan Co. (1911).

DWIGHT, THEODORE W., "Harrington and His Influence upon American Political Institutions and Political Thought," *Political Science Quarterly*, vol. II, pp. 1-44 (1887).

FARRAND, MAX, *The Framing of the Constitution of the United States*, New Haven, Yale University Press (1930).

FORD, HENRY JONES, *The Rise and Growth of American Politics*, New York, The Macmillan Co. (1914).

GAY, SIDNEY HOWARD, *James Madison*, American Statesmen Series, Edited by John T. Morse, Jr., Boston, Houghton Mifflin Co. (1892).

GREENE, EVARTS B., *The Foundations of American Nationality*, New York, American Book Co. (1922).

HILL, CHARLES E., "James Madison, Secretary of State," *The American Secretaries of State and Their Diplomacy*, Samuel F. Bemis, editor, vol. III, New York, A. A. Knopf (1927).

HOCKETT, HOMER C., *The Political and Social Growth of the United States, 1492-1852*, New York, The Macmillan Co. (1933).

HUNT, GAILLARD, *The Life of James Madison*, New York, Doubleday, Page and Co. (1902).

JACOBSON, J. MARK, *The Development of American Political Thought, A Documentary History*, New York, The Century Co. (1932).

LASKI, HAROLD J., "Democracy," *Encyclopedia of the Social Sciences*, vol. V, pp. 76-84, New York, The Macmillan Co. (1931).

MCILWAIN, C. H., *The High Court of Parliament and Its Supremacy; An Historical Essay on the Boundaries between Legislation and Adjudication in England*, New Haven, Yale University Press (1910).

MCLAUGHLIN, ANDREW C., *The Courts, the Constitution and Parties*, Chicago, The University of Chicago Press (1912).

———, *The Foundations of American Constitutionalism*, New York, New York University Press (1932).

MERRIAM, CHARLES E., *A History of American Political Theories*, New York, The Macmillan Co. (1920).

———, "The Political Theory of Jefferson," *Political Science Quarterly*, vol. XVII, pp. 24-45 (1902).

PARRINGTON, VERNON L., *Main Currents in American Thought*, three volumes, New York, Harcourt, Brace and Co. (1927).

PLUCKNETT, THEODORE F. T., "Bonham's Case and Judicial Review," *Harvard Law Review*, vol. XL, pp. 30-70 (1926).

PRATT, JULIUS W., "James Madison," *Dictionary of American Biography*, vol. XII, pp. 184-93, New York, Charles Scribner's Sons (1933).

PRATT, JULIUS W., "James Monroe, Secretary of State," *The American Secretaries of State and Their Diplomacy*, Samuel F. Bemis, editor, vol. III, New York, A. A. Knopf (1927).

———, *The Expansionists of 1812*, New York, The Macmillan Co. (1925).

RIVES, WILLIAM C., *History of the Life and Times of James Madison*, three volumes, Boston, Little, Brown and Co. (1881).

SMITH, EDWARD P., "The Movement towards a Second Constitutional Convention in 1788," *Essays in the Constitutional History of the United States in the Formative Period*, by Graduates and Former Members of the Johns Hopkins University, Edited by J. Franklin Jameson, Boston and New York, Houghton Mifflin Co. (1889).

TANSILL, CHARLES C., "Robert Smith, Secretary of State," *The American Secretaries of State and Their Diplomacy*, Samuel F. Bemis, editor, vol. III, New York, A. A. Knopf (1927).

WARREN, CHARLES, *Congress, the Constitution and the Supreme Court*, Boston, Little, Brown and Co. (1930).

———, *The Making of the Constitution*, Boston, Little, Brown and Co. (1929).

———, *The Supreme Court in United States History*, three volumes, Boston, Little, Brown and Co. (1922).

## Additional Bibliography for 1967 Edition

### PRIMARY SOURCES

HUTCHINSON, WILLIAM T., and RACHAL, WILLIAM M. E., editors, *The Papers of James Madison*, four volumes, Chicago, The University of Chicago Press (1962-1965).

### SECONDARY WORKS

BRANT, IRVING, *James Madison*, four volumes, Indianapolis, Bobbs-Merrill Co. (1941-1961).

BROWN, ROGER H., *The Republic in Peril*, New York, Columbia University Press (1965).

KOCH, ADRIENNE, *Jefferson and Madison: The Great Collaboration*, New York, Alfred A. Knopf (1950).

PERKINS, BRADFORD, *The Causes of the War of 1812*, New York, Holt, Rinehart and Winston (1962).

# Index

# Index